Heather Kapplow

111 Places
in Boston
That You Must
Not Miss

Photographs by Alyssa Wood

AG 2 6 '22

111

emons:

...lways championing my writing.

Kim Windyka

© Emons Verlag GmbH
All rights reserved
Photographs by Alyssa Wood
Cover motif: shutterstock.com/2p2play; FrimuFilms
Edited by Karen E. Seiger
Layout: Editorial Design & Artdirection, Conny Laue,
based on a design by Lübbeke | Naumann | Thoben
Maps: altancicek.design, www.altancicek.de
Basic cartographical information from Openstreetmap,
OpenStreetMap-Mitwirkende, ODbL
Printing and binding: Grafisches Centrum Cuno, Calbe
Printed in Germany 2022
ISBN 978-3-7408-1558-5
Second revised edition, January 2022

Did you enjoy this guidebook? Would you like to see more?
Join us in uncovering new places around the world on:
www.111places.com

Foreword

Boston is a bit contradictory in nature. It's seen around the world as a center of intellectual pursuits, but it's equally renowned for its rock music. Boston is known as the birthplace of the United States, but also as a land of thick accents, terrible driving, and brusque unfriendliness. It's all true. However, that just scratches the surface of our city's character. With this guidebook, we'll take you a little deeper.

Yes, we're steeped in history. Walk through Boston Common, and you'll see costumed Ben Franklins scrolling on their phones in between Freedom Trail walking tours. Just down the street, Paul Revere, Sam Adams, Crispus Attucks, and John Hancock are buried. Nearly everywhere you turn, there's a nod to our colonial and revolutionary past. But we also have enough tech innovation incubating to keep yesterday and tomorrow equally in sight. You'll find a fusion of the two realities reflected in everything from our public transit system to our culinary offerings.

In these pages, we've given you enough insider tips to catch Boston letting its guard (and hair) down, including some discoveries that were new to us as veteran Bostonians! But if you're looking for hints about where to park, we'll never tell. That's sacred knowledge that must be earned through hours of block circling, snow shoveling, and fistfuls of tickets. Are we uptight? Only if you cut us off on the Pike or dare to wear a Yankees cap.

Oh, and one more thing: we'll disappoint you with our accents because they'll never be as thick as the exaggerated imitations you've heard in the movies. Sorry about that. On the bright side, you'll find us much more welcoming – and far less thuggish – than we are on screen. "How do you like them apples?"

Please enjoy all of the cracks, crevices, secrets, and stories of Boston that we've shared with you here. We love our city, and we hope you will too.

111 Places

1 40 South Street

For those about to frock

Punks, hipsters, and lovers of funky secondhand fashion, take heed. This tiny boutique, owned by local rocker and renaissance woman Hilken Mancini, is jam-packed with handpicked, one-of-a-kind vintage styles that are just begging to be worn on stage or your next album cover. From retro graphic tees to disco-inspired dresses and chic blazers, the 1960s, 1970s, and 1980s – give or take a decade on either side – are all alive and well on the racks here.

The store existed as a shop called Gumshoe for years before being transformed into a treasure chest of coed clothing, shoes, and accessories. It all began when Mancini, who has played in local bands like Fuzzy, The Monsieurs, and Shepherdess, crossed paths with Gumshoe owner Otto Johnson, a bartender at storied Boston punk club The Rathskeller (aka "The Rat."). Johnson was using the space above the club to sell pre-owned clothing in addition to operating the space in Jamaica Plain, more of a warehouse than a store at the time. "He was only selling men's vintage out of there," Mancini recalls. "There wasn't a dressing room or any track lighting." The pair's rock and roll roots made them the perfect match, and they decided to join forces around 2005. "He liked me because I was a musician who had just lost my record deal and was figuring out ways to make money," she explains. "So I moved in and made it more of a store, and we split the rent." Since then, she has carved out a special space that fits right into the already-artsy neighborhood.

Aside from offering statement pieces and unique duds, 40 South Street doesn't just look the part; the lifestyle is in its DNA, through and through. Mancini is the creator of Punk Rock Aerobics and was a cofounder of the Girls Rock Campaign Boston, which provides music education and enrichment programs to the future Joan Jetts and Debbie Harrys of the world.

Address 40 South Street, Jamaica Plain, MA 02130, +1 (617) 522-5066, www.fortysouthst.com | **Getting there** Subway to Green Street (Orange Line) | **Hours** Thu & Fri 1–7pm, Sat 11am–6pm, Sun noon–5pm | **Tip** Want to see some technology from the same vintage as your duds? The Byte Shop, just a few doors away (48 South Street, Jamaica Plain, www.byteshop.io) has a small, quirky museum of computer history.

2 __ A4cade
Kiddin' around

What's better than a dimly-lit emporium of retro video and pinball games? A dimly-lit emporium of retro video and pinball games that serves grilled cheese sandwiches and cocktails. At Central Square's A4cade, the joint effort of beloved local restaurants Area Four and Roxy's Grilled Cheese, nostalgia and kitsch are baked into every part of the experience, whether it's the Pac-Man machine or a cheeky, Mario-inspired tiki drink called Princess Peach's Downfall. There's also an impressive selection of craft beers from area breweries and wines by the glass if you absolutely insist on acting like a grown-up.

Roxy's renowned grilled cheese sandwiches and burgers, which were born from a food truck, are the other stars of the show. This isn't your average Kraft-singles affair. Rather, you'll find dressed-up takes like the Mighty Rib Melt with a three-cheese blend, caramelized onions, and braised barbeque short rib, or the Green Muenster Melt, which combines North Country bacon and house-made guacamole. And it wouldn't be a proper party without classic burgers and hot dogs, though veggie options are also available.

If you were wondering, the games operate on the same token system you remember from those carefree days when you'd spend all afternoon furiously trying to defeat the Frogger machine, only to be rewarded with a plastic mood ring. There aren't any prizes here, but there is booze, which more than makes up for it.

For an extra dose of childhood happiness, grab a cone of vanilla soft serve or a cereal milkshake to sip while playing Mortal Kombat II and Galaga. Adding to the jovial atmosphere are near-nightly DJs spinning live and frequent events. "A4cade has no pretense or agenda – we just want to do fun stuff," says Roxy's founder and owner James DiSabatino. "From drag trivia to pinball tournaments and Area 51 parties, our vibe is just about having a good time."

Address 292 Massachusetts Avenue, Cambridge, MA 02139, +1 (617) 714-3960, www.a4cade.com, a4cade@areafour.com | Getting there Subway to Central Square (Red Line) | Hours Tue–Thu 5–11pm, Fri & Sat 5pm–1am | Tip Sort through the racks at Boomerangs (563 Massachusetts Avenue, Cambridge, www.shopboomerangs.org) to find an old-school outfit that's perfect for a leisurely day of Tetris and Skee-Ball.

3 ___ The Abiel Smith School

"O" is for Opium, "P" is for Prostitution

In 1783, Massachusetts became the first state in the US to abolish slavery. As a result, it quickly amassed the highest concentration of free Blacks in the country.

By the early 1800s, Boston was a hotbed of progressive black political activity. Writer and former slave Frederick Douglass, along with abolitionist and journalist William Lloyd Garrison, established Boston as a major stop on the touring abolitionist speaker circuit. With such a firm commitment to the raising of collective consciousness, it should come as no surprise that the first public school for free Black people in the country was founded here.

The school began in 1798 at the home of former slave and son of the founder of Black Freemasonry, Primus Hall. When it outgrew his home, it moved to the basement of the African American Meeting House. Then, in 1815, when philanthropist Abiel Smith left significant funds "for the education of Black youth" in his will, it became the Abiel Smith School, officially joining the larger American public school system in 1816. Smith's endowment allowed the construction of the current building, which opened its doors in 1835, hosting over 100 students in that first year.

But the school was not without its scandals. There were frequent complaints about the quality of the teachers assigned here compared to white schools. In particular, there were complaints that one teacher was "visiting a house of ill fame" during the school day. And now archeological evidence points to the possibility that teachers were medicating their students as much as they were educating them!

Tensions rose about the racial inequity in the city's public school system until violence erupted in 1850. By 1855, courts forced the school system to integrate, and the Abiel Smith School closed, ultimately becoming a part of the African-American History Museum.

Address 46 Joy Street, Boston, MA 02114, +1 (617) 725-0022 x330, www.maah.org/boston_campus | **Getting there** Subway to Park Street (Red or Green Line) | **Hours** Mon–Sat 10am–4pm | **Tip** The Abiel Smith School is one of many stops in the Beacon Hill area that are on Boston's African American Heritage Walking Trail. Find out more and download a map (www.maah.org/boston_heritage_trail).

4 Aerosmith Apartment

Definitely not where Love in an Elevator happened

When traveling around the world, you hear two things pretty consistently from people who have never been to Boston. One of them is that Boston is "the Athens of America" (a high – but possibly deluded – compliment). The other is that Boston has spawned some of the best rock music on the face of the planet, a compliment that is 100% spot on. Let's not quibble here about whether Aerosmith should be seen as the high point in the pantheon of rock god-and-goddess-ness that has poured forth from the city's many basements, where people were able to get away with rehearsing, and focus instead on how recognizable their name is. Since they are a very well-known Boston rock band, it makes sense to have them stand in symbolically for all of the many, many other rock bands from Boston that have blown the minds of music fans everywhere. And so it also makes sense to go on a pilgrimage to where this band began.

Like all bands that aspire to be on tour all the time and don't want to have to find individual sub-lessors, Aerosmith hit on the brilliant idea of sharing an apartment in Boston's Allston neighborhood, often referred to colloquially as "Allston Rock City," because so many other bands have done the same thing here over many decades. Just imagine how tight a band's repertoire and repartee can get if they eat all their meals together and stay up all night talking about the nuances of their songs. That's exactly what happened in this third floor brownstone walkup apartment at 1325 Commonwealth Avenue.

Joe Perry and Steven Tyler wrote their very first song here together in 1970, "Movin' Out." The band debuted the song at a Massachusetts high school and then recorded it in the apartment for their first album, "Aerosmith" – on a waterbed because their other roommate (and roadie) worked for a waterbed company. The song is actually about the apartment. Well, about moving out of it.

Aerosmith Apartment

The five original members of the rock band Aerosmith (Steven Tyler, Joe Perry, Brad Whitford, Joey Kramer, and Tom Hamilton) lived on the second story of this building in the early 1970s. It was here "The Bad Boys of Boston" began their remarkable career. "Movin' Out," a track on their self-titled debut album, was written about moving out of this apartment. Known for their oversized personalities and combustible stage performances of blues-tinged hard rock, Aerosmith went on to become one of America's most influential rock and roll bands and achieved international success.

Address 1325 Commonwealth Avenue, Allston, MA 02134 | **Getting there** Subway to Griggs Street (Green "B" Line) | **Hours** Unrestricted from the outside only | **Tip** To hear – and see – which bands the hippest Allstonians are into these days, catch a show at Brighton Music Hall (158 Brighton Avenue, Allston, www.crossroadspresents.com/pages/brighton-music-hall).

5 The Ancient Crypt

Mo' bodies, mo' problems

The North End is known for having some of the best Italian food in the city. But there are more than a thousand bone-chilling secrets lurking below those plates of linguini. In the 18th and 19th century, Boston was experiencing a serious shortage of land for burials, and desperate times called for legally and sanitarily questionable measures.

Beginning in 1732, several brick tombs – 37 in all – were built underneath the Old North Church to house coffins for those who paid a fee. However, with space at a premium, the tombs didn't stay empty for long. Despite the fact that some of these graves were privately owned, the church reused them, even dismembering skeletons to fit more bodies (a practice that seems unscrupulous now, but was common back then). Giving new meaning to "making the most of your space," a group of British soldiers who died during the Battle of Bunker Hill were packed into one tomb, and any non-parishioner who shelled out $10 could be squeezed into another. With a grand total of 1,100 bodies, you don't have to be a mathematician to conclude that these corpses were too close for comfort.

So many interred remains in such cozy quarters also led to an unpleasant odor that even the best eggplant parmigiana couldn't mask. With the addition of ventilation, the stench eventually began to seep out and threaten the health of churchgoers and neighborhood residents, causing the city to mandate that the crypt be sealed in 1853. Not wanting to lose this lucrative income stream, the church ignored the requests and kept on cryptin' until they were finally forced to end the practice once and for all in 1860.

While the tombs remain sealed for everyone's sake, you can get up close and creepy with them on the church's Behind the Scenes tour and learn more about the unlucky souls who found their final resting places in one of the hottest subterranean spots around.

Address 193 Salem Street, Boston, MA 02113, +1 (617) 858-8231, www.oldnorth.com | Getting there Subway to Haymarket (Orange or Green Line) | Hours Apr–Oct, Tue–Sat 10am–5pm; Nov–Mar, Wed–Sat 10am–4pm | Tip If the thought of all of the cold, stale bodies haven't diminished your appetite, there's some hot, fresh bread waiting for you at Bricco Panetteria (241 Hanover Street, Boston, www.briccosalumeria.com/panetteria), a hidden bakery in a narrow alley a few blocks away – just let your nose guide you.

6 Arax Market

All the ingredients for a festive feast

Even in a region as historic as New England, it can often be difficult to find many businesses that have stood the test of time, let alone a specialty ethnic food shop. Arax Market is wonderfully surprising in this way – and many other ways too.

A mom and pop shop through and through, the store was established in 1974 by Elizabeth Bassmajian, her brothers, and her husband Hagop as a way to address the frustration of not being able to find their favorite ingredients for traditional Armenian meals. Today, Bassmajian's three children, Shant, Betty, and Harout, run the show, scouring produce markets at the crack of dawn every day for fresh fruits and vegetables, stocking groceries, and arranging deliveries from specialty vendors. The tight-knit family feel at Arax extends beyond the clan and to the customers. The store has become a cornerstone of the community, drawing a diverse and loyal legion of shoppers, who rely on its rare and exhaustively sourced products, and also on its knowledgeable and personable staff.

If you have a hankering for hummus or baba ghanoush, you'll surely see it here, but Arax's more unique selections are where it really shines. We're talking creamy Armenian string cheese flecked with nigella seeds, pickled everything (including eggplant, mushrooms, and okra), and *lamejun*, a thin-crust pizza topped with minced meat and veggies. You'll also find everything you need to flex your culinary muscles, from grape leaves to pepper paste and from-scratch spices. And then there are the olives – a buffet of salty, delicious olives that would make the ones at Whole Foods cower in shame.

In the mood for something sweet? You have a couple of options: scan the case for a freshly-made pastry, like pistachio baklava. Or browse their selection of hookahs, flavored tobacco, and accessories. You may just have to throw a dinner party.

Address 585 Mount Auburn Street, No. 4154, Watertown, MA 02472, +1 (617) 924-3399 | Getting there Bus 71 to Mount Auburn Street & Upland Road | Hours Mon–Fri 9am–8pm, Sat 9am–7pm, Sun noon–4pm | Tip Continue your trip around the world with a stop for Greek goods at Sophia's Greek Pantry (265 Belmont Street, Belmont, www.sophiasgreekpantry.com).

7 Artisan's Asylum

Meet your (inner) maker

In the mood to master a new skill? Whether it's bike building, woodworking, or even assembling wearable electronics, the programs at the Asylum's 52,000-square-foot warehouse will bring out the creator within. At this non-profit, self-proclaimed "community fabrication center," all lessons are led by local artists, including specialty family classes that will get the whole gang involved.

The Asylum offers several membership options, including day passes that let you sample the goods (and the gear that makes them). Daily tours take you through some of the private artists studio spaces and workshops, where 40 to 50 classes are held each month. There's truly something for everyone: traditional pastimes like figure drawing and welding complement newer forms of expression like laser stamp making and 3D printer training. The center frequently opens its doors to the community with a speaker series and plenty of free work nights that focus on fiber arts, circuit hacking, and more. Around the holidays, its annual market gives members a chance to sell the fruits of their labor.

Gui Cavalcanti founded the Asylum in 2010 while working full-time at Boston Dynamics, an engineering and robotics design company. Initially, it was just a passion project on the side. The first iteration was a much smaller, volunteer-run space. Shortly after the team moved into a new, larger home, it became apparent that it was time for a full staff. Then this massive hub of innovation outgrew its 40,000-square-foot space in Somerville in early 2020 and moved into two overhauled former film-set storage facilities a few miles away in Brighton at the end of 2021. The spanking new space has dedicated heavy-duty and light-duty shops for those working on both big and small projects.

From finally turning that off-the-wall idea into a reality to taking the first steps towards starting a bona fide business, it's not an exaggeration to say that this is the place where dreams come true.

Address 96 Holton Street, Brighton, MA 02135, +1 (617) 284-6878, www.artisansasylum.com, general-info@artisansasylum.com | Getting there Buses 70/70A, 86, or 66 to North Harvard & Franklin Streets; Franklin Commuter Rail Line from to Brighton Landing | Hours See website for classes and open shop times | Tip If you need inspiration, pop into nearby Charles River Speedway (525 Western Avenue, Brighton, www.charlesriverspeedway.com), where a hip hodgepodge of artisan booths circle an old racing stable-turned-brewery.

8__ Backbar

Clandestine cocktails in a tiny speakeasy

Turn down a particular alley in Somerville's Union Square, look to your right, and you'll find yourself facing a barely marked metal door. Open that door, and you'll find yourself in a dim, nondescript, cement hallway with another metal door at the other end of it. Open *that* door, and you'll find yourself in Backbar, Boston's coziest speakeasy.

Only a secret for the first three months or so of its existence, Backbar has been at the top of Boston's best bars lists for several years now but still offers a thrill of discovery when you find it for the first time. If you're certain you're in the wrong place, you're in the right place. And if you manage to get there early enough, you'll not only score a comfy padded and pillowed bench seat or a barstool, but some late afternoon glow through the bar's sweet, tucked-away skylight. It's a great place to meet someone to talk about something illicit – once those two doors close behind you, you'll feel as if you've entered a zone that's been hermetically sealed off from the rest of your life.

And of course, it's a great place to get a drink. The cocktail craft is peak here, and every drink has a story and an elegant glass. The shelves above the bar glitter with exotically-shaped and labeled glass bottles, only about a third of which will look familiar to you – there is *always* a milk punch special. Backbar's milk punches are based on hand-clarified milk and any number of bourbon/brandy possibilities, plus a bit of sweetness and spice.

You'll probably get peckish for something tasty to munch on, and luckily, the bar snacks here are both artful and delectable. Sometimes they are elevated simple fare: hot dogs on brioche buns with caramelized onions; ramen with handmade noodles and pork belly. Other times, it's something from the high-end farm-to-table tasting menu of Field & Vine around the corner. All in all, a night at Backbar is about the best way a walk down a dark alley can go.

Address 7 Sanborn Court, Somerville, MA 02143, +1 (617) 718-0249, www.backbarunion.com, info@backbarunion.com | Getting there Bus 86 or 91 to Washington Street & Merriam Street | Hours Tue–Sun 5pm–midnight | Tip Prospect Hill Park, just an 8-minute walk from Backbar, offers one of the best views of the city of Boston (www.somervillema.gov/prospecthillpark).

9 Berlin Wall Chunk

A chip off the old bloc

At the entrance to the Hult International Business School in Cambridge, you'll find an unassuming concrete block featuring a fun and colorful doodle. Unless you're a major history buff, you'd likely have no idea at first glance that you were looking at a key piece of European history. From 1961 to 1989, the wall divided Berlin, Germany into two parts both symbolically and literally. Its construction came after a lengthy period of strife following World War II, when the city was first partitioned into four sections.

In 1961, it all began to hit the fan as nearly 50,000 fled from the German Democratic Republic through Berlin in June and July. On August 12, 2,400 escaped from East Germany into West Berlin, marking the highest number of refugees in one day. It was this mass exodus that prompted Soviet Premier Khrushchev to order the East German border closed once and for all. The wall was created in only 14 days by soldiers, police officers, and volunteers, and it remained there for nearly three decades until several factors, including the end of communism in Poland, led to its fall in 1989.

Hult is owned by international travel and education company Education First (EF), so the wall segment – the only full panel on free display in Massachusetts – isn't completely out of nowhere. In fact, EF had an office in West Germany for several years, and opened an office in East Berlin the day after the Wall's demise. The piece was presented to EF founder Bertil Hult for his 50th birthday at a ceremony that was attended by Senator Edward Kennedy.

"The segment that sits on our campus has always served as a powerful reminder of EF's mission of opening the world through education and how the programs we offer help break down barriers of language, culture, and geography and spark mutual understanding," says Brooke Parker, Growth Marketing Manager at EF.

Address 1 Education Street, Cambridge, MA 02141, +1 (617) 746-1990, www.hult.edu |
Getting there Subway to Community College (Orange Line) or Lechmere (Green "E" Line) |
Hours Unrestricted | Tip Find a historical souvenir that you can actually take home
at the Cambridge Antique Market, a multilevel complex featuring a variety of vendors
(201 Monsignor O'Brien Highway, Cambridge, www.marketantique.com/cambridg.htm).

10 Blackfriars Massacre Site

The hits just kept on coming

Boston is rife with Irish pubs, but how many were the site of the most gruesome murders the city has ever seen? Today, you'll find a sleek, mixed-use retail and office building where The Blackfriars Pub once stood – a far cry from the spot's former life as an after-hours hotspot and sordid hotbed of nefarious mob activity that likely saw its fair share of both guns and cannolis.

On June 28, 1978, it was business as usual for the bar and dance club until the drug-fueled disco antics died down for the evening. Custodian Jerry Robinson encountered the grisly scene at 8am as he entered a tiny office in the basement. There, where five men had been playing backgammon in between arranging drug deals and committing bankruptcy fraud, were their lifeless, bloody bodies, scattered around the room like dice. According to investigators, they'd all been shot around 2am by a .25 caliber semi-automatic pistol, then two sawed-off shotguns. The victims were identified as club owner Vincent Solmonte, club manager and local news anchor John (Jack) Kelly, and their pals Peter Meroth, Freddie Delavega, and Charles Magarian.

Solmonte was identified as a potential target. Not only was he a well-known cocaine trafficker, but he was deep in debt and under investigation by the FBI and IRS. Reporter Jack Kelly had embedded himself with some shady characters in pursuit of better sources, however, which also raised some eyebrows about his associations.

And who pulled the triggers? You don't have to know much about Boston to know that there's one name synonymous with organized crime in the city: Whitey Bulger. While the head honcho of the Winter Hill Gang was never able to be placed at the scene – in fact, nobody was ever convicted – let's just say he knew a couple of guys. Robert Italiano and William Ierardi were tried and acquitted in 1979, though Stephen Flemmi and Nicholas Femia were rumored to be involved.

Address 105 Summer Street, Boston, MA 02111 | Getting there Subway to Downtown Crossing (Orange or Red Line), Park Street (Green Line), or State Street (Blue Line) | Hours Unrestricted | Tip Channel the incognito vibes of mafiosos past without all of those pesky arrest warrants at dimly lit cocktail bar jm Curley (21 Temple Place, Boston, www.jmcurleyboston.com). Then, sneak into its secret back room steakhouse, Bogie's Place, for a grass-fed filet mignon or dry-aged tomahawk.

11 Bodega

Get your kicks... behind a fake vending machine

Hidden away behind an unassuming convenience store façade in the heart of Back Bay is Bodega, a small yet mighty wonderland of urban apparel and sneakers that's been exclusive by design since its opening in 2006. Only those visitors savvy enough to navigate past the sundries, snacks, and cleaning supplies will discover a secret passageway – cleverly disguised as a Snapple vending machine – that will transport them into the sleek boutique and grant them access to the latest goods from more than 100 of the world's top streetwear brands. That's right; there's no advertising or signage on the storefront, so Bodega owes the majority of its success to word-of-mouth, local press coverage, and a fiercely loyal base of return customers. Don't even bother trying to call them either because a place this far under the radar is definitely too cool to have a telephone.

Even if you're not a "sneakerhead," or footwear aficionado, the inherent chicness of the space and knowledgeable, passionate staff just might have you worshipping at the altar of Converse and Common Projects by the time you make your way out of the veritable high-top heaven and back into the real world.

It's not all kicks, either. You'll also find clothing from the likes of Maison Kitsuné, Brain Dead, and Parra, plus the latest caps and accessories to complete your head-to-toe look. The merchandise is all expertly curated and frequently refreshed by co-owners Jay Gordon, Oliver Mak, and Dan Natola, so you'll likely get a unique experience with each visit. To be certain, this isn't the least expensive boutique in town, but, hey, as the saying goes, it costs to be cool.

And if you also happen to be in need of toilet paper or a soft drink, you can snag those and other corner store-type products before you go. The trick bodega might be mostly intended as a decoy, but fortunately, it isn't completely for show.

Address 6 Clearway Street, Boston, MA 02115, shop.bdgastore.com | **Getting there** Subway to Back Bay (Orange Line) or Symphony (Green "E" Line); bus 1 to Massachusetts Avenue & Boylston Street | **Hours** Sun–Wed noon–6pm, Thu–Sat noon–7pm | **Tip** Grab a craft beer and some nachos at Bukowski Tavern (50 Dalton Street, Boston, www.bukowski-tavern.com), a cash-only dive that's steps from the upscale Prudential Center, yet worlds away in its grungy, no-frills vibe.

12 _ Boston Barber & Tattoo Co.

Where buzz cuts meet body art

Go in for a trim and a shave; leave with some brand new ink. That's the unexpected beauty of this hybrid barbershop and tattoo studio, the only one of its kind in the Boston area.

"Every neighborhood has a heartbeat," explains owner Robert Dello Russo. "A place that represents the cultural epicenter of the area at its core." And in his estimation, no place better encompasses the vibrant, warm spirit of the North End than his shop. In a tight-knit community like this, where the roots run deep and traditions are held close, there are more than a few fixtures that act as more of a gathering place than a business. Neighbors become like family. As an old-fashioned barber shop with a modern twist, spots like this one are the best of both worlds.

Sure, you'll find the standard services, like hot shaves, beard trims, and buzz cuts, but you can also walk on the wild side with a custom tattoo by one of the experienced artists on hand. Believe it or not, the tattoo shop here has been the sole studio in downtown Boston for 50 years. Actually, if you know anything about the city and its notoriously Puritanical roots, that might not come as too much of a surprise. Happy hours are still illegal in Massachusetts, after all.

Not only does Boston Barber draw die-hard locals, but it's also attracted famous clients throughout the years, including Bruin Brad Marchand and former Celtic Gordon Hayward. And because this is Little Italy, there's an espresso and coffee bar if you need to steel yourself for the pain of your impending body art, or just get an extra jolt of caffeinated confidence. Can't make it to the North End? You won't be able to get a tat, but an outpost in Beacon Hill offers the same barber services and neighborhood feel.

Address 113 Salem Street, Boston, MA 02113, +1 (617) 742-0611, www.bostonbarber.com, info@bostonbarber.com | **Getting there** Subway to Haymarket (Orange or Green Line) | **Hours** Mon 11am–8pm, Tue & Wed 10am–7pm, Thu & Fri 10am–8pm, Sat 9am–4pm | **Tip** Self-care also comes in the form of food; treat yourself to a warm lobster roll or the on-point raw bar specialties at Neptune Oyster (63 Salem Street, No. 1, Boston, www.neptuneoyster.com).

13 Boston Cyberarts Gallery
Catch a glimpse of the future before your train

Filled with high-tech pieces from both local and international artists, the cutting-edge Boston Cyberarts Gallery is tucked quietly into the Green Street subway station in Jamaica Plain (JP). It holds the delightfully quirky distinction of being the only art gallery in a train station in the entire country. Rotating exhibits run the gamut from animation to sound vibrations, letting you experience the advancements that are shaping both new media – and our world. Most of them are designed to make you consider technology and its broader impact, incorporating apps and virtual reality experiences, while others are just really fun to look at and interact with – like playing video games to create your own poetry.

Behind all of the LCD screens and pixel art is The Boston Cyberarts Organization, a nonprofit also headquartered in JP. It was originally created in 1999 to put on a now-defunct festival. "The group has been exploring the intersections of art and technology with exhibitions at the Boston Cyberarts Gallery, the Art on the Marquee project at the Boston Convention and Exhibition Center, and through numerous public art projects of both actual and augmented reality," says Executive Director George Fifield.

After the gallery, formerly called the Axiom Center for New and Experimental Media, closed in 2012, Boston Cyberarts kept the space alive. The gallery is free and hosts frequent receptions for exhibits focused on themes like nostalgia, data visualization, neural networks, and more. Artists often enhance their work at these events with live performances, including dance or spoken word.

If you can't drop by during the gallery's operating hours, you can still get your futuristic fix after the T is closed for the evening. From lasers to colorful video clips, the floor-to-ceiling windows make it easy to see what's inside – and what lies ahead.

Address 141 Green Street, Jamaica Plain, MA 02130, +1 (617) 522-6710, www.bostoncyberarts.org | Getting there Subway to Green Street (Orange Line) | Hours Fri–Sun noon–6pm | Tip After beaming forward in time, press rewind with an indie DVD from the Video Underground (3203 Washington Street, Jamaica Plain, www.thevideounderground.com), the only remaining rental store in the area. The VU regularly hosts public screenings of old favorites and cult classics.

14 Boston Hassle Flea

The coolest crafts around

Treat yourself to a one-of-a-kind, subcultural souvenir (or three) from this roaming pop-up market, hosted by DIY arts organization, Boston Hassle. Every other month, local vendors come together in a different community center to mingle and sell all sorts of handmade treasures, from art to zines and just about everything in between. In this case, "everything" might refer to earrings made of computer parts, glass cauldrons, witty laptop stickers, or a wreath that juxtaposes colorful flowers with animal bones.

It's not unusual to find an item for sale here that's so creative, you actually have to ask the vendor to identify it for you. Most of the time, it's safe to assume that it's a bong, but not always. As much a lively gathering place as a showcase for emerging artists, half the fun is coming back throughout the years and seeing both fresh faces and fresh creations from returning sellers. Plus, there's almost always coffee from an area café on hand to fuel your hunt for artisanal knick-knacks.

The Flea is also a fantastic place to find some truly unique vintage clothing and accessories that will help you rock a devil-may-care punk teenager look – or just help you live out those fantasies if you were more ho-hum than hooligan. We're talking lots of studs, leather, patches, rips, and safety pins that would certainly evoke an "I'm not mad, I'm just disappointed" reaction from your mother and possibly get you sent to detention. Along with the wackier goods are slightly tamer items that make for great gifts, like ceramics, body products, vinyl records, houseplants, and loose leaf tea.

You'll find offerings of the more experiential variety here, too, including live drawings and caricatures, tarot readings, and even on-site haircuts if you're really in the mood to reinvent your entire look. On the fence about chopping off your locks? You can always consult the cards first.

Address Various, www.bostonhassle.com/bostonhassleflea, bostonhassle@gmail.com | Getting there See website for locations | Hours See website for schedule | Tip When this flea market happens to be in Cambridge's Central Square, which it often is, complete your eclectic day by checking in at the outdoor cultural space, Starlight Square (84 Bishop Allen Drive, Cambridge, www.starlightsquare.org).

15 Bully Boy Distillers

Whiskey business

In a city full of breweries, Roxbury's Bully Boy Distillers shows some much-deserved love to whiskey, rum, gin, vodka, and amaro. Brothers Will and Dave Willis established their craft distillery – Boston's first – in 2010, inspired by their childhood on a fourth-generation working farm in Sherborn, MA. Initially, the two brewed cider, eventually moving on to brandy and other spirits. Their passion was further nurtured when they discovered a hidden vault in the basement of the farmhouse. It was here that they found not only a secret world of forgotten booze, but also the name of the distillery.

Along with all kinds of liquor was a perplexing plaque dedicated to one of the horses on the farm named Bully Boy. The brothers did a bit of investigating and found out two things: one, that their great-grandfather was good friends with Teddy Roosevelt! Two, that the horse's moniker stemmed from one of Teddy Roosevelt's favorite expressions, "Bully!" which they learned was a synonym for extraordinary. Once the name was decided, they built the brand from the ground up, going door to door at bars and meticulously monitoring their product for taste and quality, a process that continues today.

It paid off. After a handful of years in their original location, Bully Boy moved into its current 8,000 square-foot space across the street in 2015. They offer public tours that let you see exactly how the magic happens and catch a glimpse of the two massive stills where the gin (and everything else) is stored.

There's a stylish tasting room with a full bar, complete with flights of old fashioneds, Moscow mules, and daiquiris, plus specialty drinks, like Don't Call Me Shirley and Weezy's Sipper. Want to try your own hand at mixology? Take a class with one of the expert bartenders, who will share skills that you can keep in your back pocket for whenever a martini craving hits.

Address 44 Cedric Street, Roxbury, MA 02119, +1 (617) 442-6000, www.bullyboydistillers.com, info@bullyboydistillers.com | Getting there Subway to Andrew (Red Line) | Hours Thu & Fri 5–11pm, Sat 1–11pm | Tip Just imagine sipping on a gin fizz at the Shirley-Eustis House (33 Shirley Street, Roxbury, www.shirleyeustishouse.org), a historic mansion where the former Royal Governor of the Province of Massachusetts Bay William Shirley spent his summers in the mid-1700s.

16 Cambridge School of Culinary Arts

Up your romantic dinner (or breakfast) game

Though there is no shortage of incredible restaurants to go out to on a date in Boston, there will inevitably come a day in any relationship where you will need to eat something together at home. And then what? You're totally screwed. Unless you're a naturally gifted chef or you've discovered this place.

Cambridge School of Culinary Arts, staffed by some of Boston's most popular chefs, teaches techniques and cuisines that can take your home cooking (and eating) to the next level and beyond. Just want to make great eggs? They've got your back. Want to learn the basics of grilling or creating sublime sauces for things? There's a class for that. Want to take things way over the top and intimidate someone into loving you with a 15-layer foam cake with alternating layers of mousse, buttercream and ganache? Probably possible here. You can also learn about wine pairing; making pub food at home; how to make your own pasta, pickles, infused oils, and sausages from scratch; and how to cook specialties from about 15 different countries. Gluten-free, vegetarian, and locavore cooking workshops are also available, if you need them.

The School of Culinary Arts has courses especially for couples so you can learn how to cook together, and instructors can also help you learn to design romantic meals for a date or other special occasions. If things get serious, you can quickly learn the basics of preparing family holiday meals. Here are three words for you from their Christmas cooking class to get you salivating any time of year: "cherry pistachio biscotti."

If you wind up raising children together, you can make sure that they learn to cook the basics and even some impressive dishes themselves by signing them up for special after-school teen cooking lessons.

Address 2020 Massachusetts Avenue, Cambridge, MA 02140, +1 (617) 354-2020, www.cambridgeculinary.com | Getting there Subway (Red Line) to Porter | Hours See website for schedule | Tip If you find that upping your cooking game requires that you up your kitchenware game, you're in luck. Just down the block is an amazing discount houseware and party supply store, China Fair (2100 Massachusetts Avenue, Cambridge, www.chinafairinc.com).

17__Capoeira Angola

Where dancing = dueling

The Boston area has a very large Brazilian population, which is a real treat because it means that delicious Brazilian restaurants are to be found in unlikely places. And once per year, there's an out-of-this-world carnival festival featuring surreal costume parades through the streets, wild music and dancing, and yes, you guessed it, stall after stall of Brazilian street food vendors!

Brazilians have also brought a unique style of dancing/martial art called *Capoeira* to the city, and it's accessible at several different levels. *Capoeira*, best described as "a martial art hidden in dance," was transported to Brazil by African slaves in the 1500s, and was taught in clandestine ways during slavery. After slavery was abolished in Brazil in the late-1880s, *Capoeira* was outlawed but still practiced in secret in the streets of the country's poorest neighborhoods, or *favelas*.

Dancers tumble in slow or rhythmic motion with limbs intertwining and separating as they move around in a circle. It's mesmerizing to watch. The practice has its own style of music, which, like the dance, does double duty: it keeps the pace, but the words of the songs transmit *Capoeira*'s philosophy of life. Historically at least, this artform is as much political activity as it is entertainment.

And it's also a serious workout! The Dance Complex in Cambridge, which offers a wide range of multicultural dance lessons, hosts *Capoeira* classes three times a week, taught by Mestre Chuvisco, one of New England's most esteemed *Capoeira* artists, and founder of Boston's oldest *Capoeira* schools, Capoeira MdP. Mestre Chuvisco started practicing his art at 8 years old and earned the title of Mestre (Master) at the tender age of 15. He's taught thousands of students in the US and Brazil, more than 40 graduating as Mestres. So you'll be in excellent and highly experienced hands for your training in this expressive artform at The Dance Complex.

Address The Dance Complex, 536 Massachusetts Avenue, Cambridge, MA 02139, +1 (617) 547-9363, www.capoeira-angola.com | **Getting there** Subway to Central (Red Line) | **Hours** See website for seasonal schedule | **Tip** If you love all things Brazilian, keep your eye out for the colorful annual Cambridge Carnival that parades right by The Dance Complex every September. It's about the most fun you can have in the streets of Boston and has a heavy Brazilian influence (www.cambridgecarnival.org).

18 Casa Portugal

A taste of the Iberian Peninsula

It's a little known fact that Massachusetts has the largest population of people with Portuguese ancestry in the entire country. So it should come as no surprise that there are fantastic Portuguese bakeries and specialty groceries scattered all over the state. Nor should it be a surprise if you turn a corner in a suburb on a spring or late summer weekend and discover yourself in the middle of a *Festa do Divino Espirito Santo* (Feast of the Holy Spirit) or a Madeiran wine festival replete with folk dancing, a parade, and of course, Madeira wine.

The Portuguese community in the Boston area has a strong spirit of hospitality and takes great care in the preparation of food. You'll find many small Portuguese-owned restaurants preparing meals with herbs clipped from their owners' home gardens, and serving home-made wines or cordials at certain times of year.

Casa Portugal, which has been around since 1976, is one such spot. Just a touch more elegant than The Neighborhood, Somerville's beloved Portuguese breakfast joint, Casa Portugal is right over the line in Cambridge, but it feels truly Old World. White tablecloths, heavy wooden chairs, a small TV over a tiny bar, and always, always families spanning generations at pushed-together tables.

The ambience is like stepping right onto the Iberian Peninsula, and the food is melt-in-your mouth Portuguese home cooking. Try the appetizers for sure, like *ameijoas á bulhão pato* (littleneck clams in shells with garlic, olive oil, parsley and wine), or *favas com chouriço* (fava beans with spicy Portuguese sausage). Then you'll have to make some very serious choices in terms of main courses because they are all delicious, but also very hearty. Whether you choose a *bacalhau* or the *escalopes de vitela*, make sure you leave room for a flaky pastry or rich custardy dessert and a steaming *bica* (not to be confused with its less subtle cousin, espresso).

Address 1200 Cambridge Street, Cambridge, MA 02139, +1 (617) 491-8880, www.restaurantcasaportugal.com | Getting there Subway to Central (Red Line) | Hours Mon–Thu 11:30am–10pm, Fri & Sat 11:30am–11pm, Sun noon–10pm | Tip Inspired to recreate your Portuguese dessert? Meander a few blocks east and check out Elmendorf Baking Supplies. They'll have everything you need (594 Cambridge Street, Cambridge, www.elmendorfbaking.com).

19   Charles River Museum

Find out why you're totally screwed

Alice's white rabbit is typically portrayed in a bottomless suit and shirt, with his watch held aloft in front of him, crying out anxiously about how late he is. The white rabbit is us – but only because of that watch. Without his watch, he – and perhaps all of us – would just be hanging around without pants on, not worrying about anything at all.

You can thank folks like the Waltham Watch Company for the kind of anxiety that makes rabbits (and the rest of us) rush all the time. Before this era in precision watch development, no two watches kept exactly the same time, and people were not always stressed about being late.

The Waltham Watch Company, founded in Waltham, Massachusetts in 1850, was among the ten earliest watch brands in the world. Waltham Watch Company is older than Rolex. Even President Abraham Lincoln sported a Waltham watch. To this day, Waltham is known as "Watch City" in celebration of its contributions to the important field of getting us all to work relatively on time.

Abe's watch is at the Smithsonian Institution. But the machine that made the screws that made the mass production of the kind of watch that he wore possible is at The Charles River Museum of Industry & Innovation. "Charles Vander Woerd's Automatic Screw Machine," a still-operational chain of gears and belts, is the world's very first automatic lathe for making tiny watch screws. The machine makes the watches possible, and watches make the stress possible. So this early machine for making machines is worth coming to see, just so you know what to curse next time you're stuck in traffic.

Beyond the screw machine, the museum is a beautiful maze of ancient pocket watches, vintage voltage meters, and other fascinating industrial doodads sited in an old mill atop the winding Charles River. In fact, it's rather a wonderland for curious people of all ages.

Address 154 Moody Street, Waltham, MA 02453, +1 (781) 893-5410, www.charlesrivermuseum.org, info@charlesrivermuseum.org | Getting there Bus 70 to Carter Street & Waltham Station; Fitchburg Commuter Rail to Waltham | Hours See website for current programming | Tip Can't get enough of the gears? 10,000+ other people feel the same way and gather annually at the Watch City Steampunk Festival (Waltham Commons, www.watchcityfestival.com), donning their finest cogs and making quite a spectacle.

20 Christian Herter Park
A hidden world in plain sight

The Charles River has one very famous amphitheater – the Hatch Shell – where half a million Bostonians convene to watch 4th of July fireworks every year. But it also has a smaller amphitheater a few miles down the river that's a well-kept secret because it was completely abandoned for many years.

Christian Herter Park, an untended rose garden featuring a circular marble memorial bench, is dedicated to career politician (and Freemason) Christian Herter (1895 – 1966). It's a quaint, shady spot that is perfect for picnics or contemplation.

The park is flanked by two structures left over from a failed cultural vision for Boston called The Metropolitan Boston Arts Center. The Arts Center started off with promise: on opening day, VIPs arrived by boat, and the paparazzi had a literal field day. But it ended in shame. Half of the center's features were never realized, it was too far from public transit, and there was a pesky corruption scandal.

Still, the artifacts remain. Behind the Herter memorial is an amazing piece of modernist architecture, glass-enclosed and sitting atop 12-foot cement posts, that was home to Boston's Institute of Contemporary Art twice in the 1960s. The museum moved constantly during this decade, but the building, designed by the museum's founder, was intended as its forever-home. But alas, it was too far from mass transit to draw the hoped-for crowds.

On the other side of the garden is a 350-seat, open-air theater. Originally, it had round canvas walls and an inflated domed roof. But the roof and theater were plagued with logistical and political problems and ultimately, a fire. In 2017, a community group restored it, dubbing it The Christian Herter Amphitheater. On summer weekends, it hosts free punk rock and experimental jazz shows, 1980s classic movie nights, *Rocky Horror Picture Show* singalongs and stand-up comedy.

Address 1175 Soldiers Field Road, Allston, MA 02134, www.friendsofherterpark.org, info@herterpark.org | **Getting there** Subway to Harvard (Red Line); bus 86 to Western Avenue & Everett Street (Reservoir) | **Hours** Daily dawn–dusk, see website for events | **Tip** On a sunny day, take a kayak out on the river from the dock right next to Herter Park (www.paddleboston.com/rentals).

21 Church of the Covenant

Glitz, glam, and God

It seems only fitting that a church with a lavish interior designed by Tiffany & Co. sits pretty on Newbury Street, Boston's ritziest shopping thoroughfare. Erected in 1867 and designed by Richard M. Upjohn, the stunning Gothic Revival-style structure actually boasts the largest Tiffany stained glass windows in the entire country. There are 42 of them in all, in jewel-tone hues that illuminate the space with colorful natural light. Its pews and steeple towers, at 240 feet surpassing even the iconic Bunker Hill Monument, are made of black walnut.

The non-denominational church, which was born of a union between the Central Congregational and First Presbyterian Church in 1931, has long and widely been regarded for its beauty. In his 1892 book *One Hundred Days in Europe*, Oliver Wendell Holmes commented, "We have one steeple in Boston that to my eyes seems absolutely perfect – that of the Central Church on the corner of Newbury and Berkeley streets."

A complete redesign of the space, overseen by J. A. Holzer of The Tiffany Company, was undertaken in the 1890s. Among the updates were a brand new baptismal font, a fresh coat of paint, and revamped arches. However, the statement piece is an elaborate, stunning chandelier that was on display at the 1893 Chicago World's Fair and donated by church patron Joseph H. White. A grand Welte-Tripp organ, featuring more than 3,500 pipes, was installed in 1929. The organ can actually replicate sounds of many different instruments, including the French horn and the harp.

The sanctuary's 15 minutes of fame came in 1999, when it was featured in the movie *Boondock Saints* as the worship space of choice for Norman Reedus' and Sean Patrick Flanery's characters. In addition to its multiple weekly masses, Church of the Covenant offers public guided tours twice a week that will walk you through its rich history.

Address 67 Newbury Street, Boston, MA 02116, +1 (617) 266-7480, www.cotcbos.org |
Getting there Subway to Arlington (Green Line) | Hours See website for hours and events |
Tip Get a taste of life in the early 20th century with a tour of the Gibson House Museum
(137 Beacon Street, Boston, www.thegibsonhouse.org), a three-generation family home that's
been meticulously preserved to tell the story of Bostonians past.

22 Club Passim

For folk's sake

Aside from being music legends, what do Bob Dylan, Joan Baez, Joni Mitchell, and Muddy Waters have in common? OK – we won't make you guess: they've all performed at Club Passim, the long standing folk club nestled in the basement of an unassuming brick building in Harvard Square. The venue, which opened in 1958 as Club 47, spent its first five years on nearby Mount Auburn Street and hosted mostly jazz performers. That is, when it wasn't being shut down by the cops for repeatedly breaking a bizarre law that wouldn't allow more than three stringed instruments to be played in an establishment that served food and beverages. The law is now gone, and you can safely enjoy salads, burgers, and brunch while tapping your toes.

While it now hosts more than 400 shows each year, Passim has managed to retain a funky, intimate atmosphere that brings music lovers face to face with their favorite singer-songwriters. The club's "campfire. festival" is a highly anticipated annual event, showcasing up-and-coming artists in a free-flowing, in-the-round environment that promotes collaboration and improvisation among musicians and audience members. It began in 1998 as a last-ditch effort to fill the typically quiet Labor Day Weekend and has since been the launching pad for popular acts, such as The Weepies and Margaret Glaspy.

In 2000, the club established its very own music school to educate and nurture the Janice Ians and Woody Guthries of tomorrow, offering lessons in guitar, fiddle, song development, and more. And its Iguana Music Fund grants about $40,000 each year to individual musicians to help them pursue their projects and passions. "Club Passim is one of the longest running venues in the country," says Managing Director Matt Smith. "Through three distinct eras (Club 47, Passim, Club Passim) it has always been a place where both talent and community are fostered."

Address 47 Palmer Street, Cambridge, MA 02138, +1 (617) 492-7679, www.passim.org, info@passim.org | Getting there Subway to Harvard (Red Line) | Hours Mon–Fri 6:30–11pm, Sat & Sun 10am–11pm | Tip Nothing quite compares to the thrill of live music, but the warmth of vinyl comes pretty close. Sort through the stacks at Planet Records (144 Mount Auburn Street, Cambridge, www.planet-records.com), where classic LPs mingle with the latest indie fare.

23 __ Cochituate Standpipe
Far up, far out

The Cochituate Standpipe, a whimsical water tower built in 1869 in the Gothic Revival style, is as fascinating as the community that formed around it. The site was originally home to a Revolutionary War fort. Once the tower was constructed, it supplied neighborhood residents with water from Natick. After the annexation of Roxbury, the structure was forgotten until 1895, when Frederick Law Olmsted's firm undertook a restoration effort, adding a balcony and returning the tower to its original shape.

Seven decades later, the standpipe was the center of a fascinating web of drugs and drama. Mel Lyman, a musician, self-proclaimed deity, and author of the book *Autobiography of a World Savior*, began the Fort Hill Community in 1963 after meeting a group of fringe folks (including psychologist and writer Timothy Leary) and discovering the mind-altering effects of LSD. Calling themselves "The Lyman Family," the members – 100 adults and 60 kids – lived in a group of homes that still surround the tower today. In 1967, they began a countercultural magazine called *Avatar*, which was a mouthpiece for Lyman's philosophical ramblings. It was highly controversial, covering themes like astrology and anti-Vietnam War sentiments.

To the outside world, this was a cult. Comparisons to the Manson family abounded, though there weren't any tales as chilling from Fort Hill. That's not to say there wasn't scandal. Actor Mark Frechette was one of the best-known family members, due to his leading role in the 1970 Antonioni film *Zabriskie Point* and botched bank robbery.

While the standpipe's balcony is only open to the public once in a blue moon, it's more than worth a visit to Highland Park to sit under a weeping willow tree, take in the neighborhood's historic architecture, and imagine the stories this majestic landmark would tell if water towers could talk.

Address 22-98 Fort Avenue, Roxbury, MA 02119 | Getting there Subway to Jackson Square (Orange Line) | Hours Unrestricted | Tip Channel the spirit of the 1960s by learning to make totally trippy looking vases, windchimes, and bowls of all varieties at Diablo Glass School (123 Terrace Street, Boston, www.diabloglassschool.com).

24 Cocoanut Grove Tragedy

Where the hottest spot in town burned down

In the 1920s, nightclubs were illegal in Boston, but "supper clubs" were somehow able to fly under the wire. The Cocoanut Grove Supper Club opened in 1927 and did a brisk business through the Prohibition era.

The vision of big band musicians Mickey Alpert and Jacques Renard, The Grove initially adhered to liquor laws but quickly went underwater. The club was bought out by bootlegger Charles "King" Solomon, who converted it to a speakeasy and underworld haven. When Solomon was gunned down, ownership went to his lawyer, Barnett Welansky, who, in addition to working for gangsters, was quite tight with the city's then mayor and so skirted around building code compliance. Superficially, The Cocoanut Grove cleaned up its act. The décor went tiki to match the name, and one of the founders was brought back in to manage the entertainment. But the remodel was cheaply done by unlicensed laborers, and many club employees were underaged and underpaid. Still, by the time night clubs were legal, The Cocoanut Grove was the swingingest place in Boston.

Then, on the fateful night of November 28, 1942, with about 1,000 people inside, the club caught fire.

The exact chain of events is not fully known, but it included a faulty light, a highly flammable artificial palm tree, and a badly installed HVAC system. The fire was catastrophic. 492 people died – a number exceeding the club's legal capacity. And the carnage was gruesome. Though some died in area hospitals, overwhelmed by the number of injured they received that night, many fatalities were people crushed in crowds trying desperately to get out. The doors had been nailed closed to keep patrons from sneaking out without paying for drinks.

The commemorative plaque embedded in the sidewalk was installed by the fire's youngest survivor in 1993. It's a somber reminder of the tragedy, as is Boston's strict Fire Prevention Code.

Address 17 Piedmont Street, Boston, MA 02116, www.cocoanutgrove.org/project | Getting there Subway to Arlington or Boylston Street (Green Line), or Tufts Medical Center (Orange Line) | Hours Unrestricted | Tip The oldest (and by far the best) drag club in Boston, Jacques Cabaret, is right across the street from the plaque and has live entertainment seven days a week (79 Broadway, Boston, www.jacques-cabaret.com).

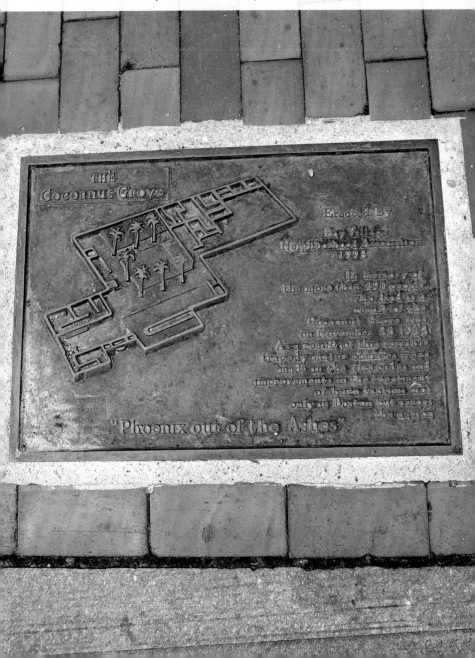

25 Coit Observatory

Somewhere, out there, beyond the pale moonlight

We all have a tendency to get caught up in the minutia of our own lives, and sometimes we need to step back and get a little bit of a wider perspective in order to see things more clearly. There is no wider perspective than that of the sky above, so next time your world is feeling small, try taking a more universal view of it through one of the telescopes at Boston University's Coit Observatory.

Every Wednesday night, if weather permits, Coit hosts Public Open Nights on the roof of their College of Arts and Sciences for the planet-curious. Astronomy students and faculty share telescope access and narrate a guided view of the night sky. From here, you can see details of the Moon, and at some times of the year Venus, Saturn, Mars, Jupiter (and Europa!), and, of course, the many constellations of the Milky Way. You also always get a great view of Boston.

It's a romantic place to go on a date. Snuggle up for the view if it's cold, enjoy the warm breeze and the night sky together if it's not, and try to find each other's astrological signs in the heavens.

Stargazing is also a great activity for families. Tear your kids' eyes away from all of the screens they always stare at, and get them out in the open air. Astronomy details offered by the observatory guides are given at a simple enough level for kids to follow, and since the Earth is always turning, what they'll see and learn about will always be different every time they come for a visit.

One important caveat: plan your trip here ahead. Look at the website or call before going, in case there is a weather-related cancellation. It's hard to see the stars if the sky is hazy or it's raining, and it's a bit hard to find your way to the roof your first time. Follow the directions on their website carefully, and don't forget to sign up in advance online (five tickets per person maximum). Arrive a little bit early, as they lock the doors once the program begins.

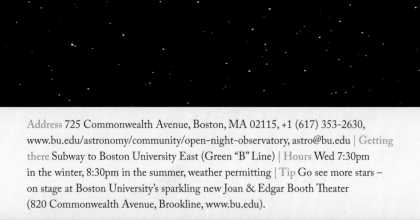

Address 725 Commonwealth Avenue, Boston, MA 02115, +1 (617) 353-2630, www.bu.edu/astronomy/community/open-night-observatory, astro@bu.edu | Getting there Subway to Boston University East (Green "B" Line) | Hours Wed 7:30pm in the winter, 8:30pm in the summer, weather permitting | Tip Go see more stars – on stage at Boston University's sparkling new Joan & Edgar Booth Theater (820 Commonwealth Avenue, Brookline, www.bu.edu).

26 Colonnade Rooftop Pool
Sun and splash in the sky

Picture this: it's steaming hot in the city, and the beaches are crammed. You're walking through Copley Square, and everyone you pass on the sidewalk is glistening with sweat. Cars are honking in standstill rush hour traffic, and the streets are wavy with heat. But you – you are keeping your cool, turning the corner onto Huntington Avenue and waltzing into the Colonnade Hotel as if you lived there. You take in a deep, air-conditioned breath as the elevator arrives, and you step into it to be taken up to the rooftop with a fabulous view of the city. You stretch, feeling the breeze that isn't available at street level brush against your skin, and then you strip off your street clothes to reveal the bathing suit you've been wearing underneath, and you dive immediately into a cool blue pool, where only a few others are doing lazy laps. With each stroke, you'll glance up at the lovely sky.

Sounds amazing, right? This could be you! You could be up in the sky, above the city's traffic and grime, swimming or lounging on a beach chair with a cocktail in your hand. And you don't even need to stay at the hotel – you just need to know, as not many people do, that their pool is open to the general public for a fee. Starting around Memorial Day every year, hotel guests and up to three friends at a time can visit the pool for free all day long, any day. The general public can buy an all-day pass for $45 per person on weekdays, or come in from 5pm onwards for $20 per person. If you want to go all out, you can rent a luxurious private cabana – pricing is a bit complicated, but it starts with a daily rental fee and a minimum food charge. Your cabana can host up to six people.

Evening public pool access is adults only (21+), and the poolside bar serves food and drink all day. It may seem a bit pricey to go regularly, but what a wonderful place for a summer birthday gathering, a never-forget-mid-summer date, or a self-care treat.

Address 120 Huntington Avenue, Boston, MA 02116, +1 (617) 425-3408, www.colonnadehotel.com/roof-top-pool | Getting there Subway to Copley (Green Line), Prudential (Green "E" Line), or Back Bay (Orange Line) | Hours Memorial Day–Labor Day, Mon–Fri 8am–10pm | Tip Check out the Christian Science Plaza Reflecting Pool (www.plaza.christianscience.com/main-landing). You can't swim in it, but it's lovely to stroll along and gaze into all 1.5 million gallons of it!

27 __ The Coolidge After Dark

Get reel weird

Sure, you can catch a plain ol' matinee at the beloved non-profit indie cinema in Brookline. But there's something undeniably exciting, vaguely dangerous, and a bit romantic about the "Coolidge After Midnite" showings of cult classics, like *The Room* and *Reefer Madness*. In this buzzy environment, it's not only acceptable to shout lines at the screen; it's encouraged.

The history of the Coolidge dates back to 1933, when the former Beacon Universalist Church was given new life as a 1,500-seat art deco theater during the Great Depression. It was a hard-fought battle to reach this point, as the town of Brookline feared that the introduction of movies into the neighborhood would be an unsavory influence on the area's youth. (The kissing and candy smuggling horror!) However, in the 1970s, the emerging popularity of mall cinemas forced the theater to differentiate itself from run-of-the-mill multiplexes. Justin Freed took charge in 1977, reimagining the theater as an arthouse concept that ran revivals and classics along with new releases.

Ever since, it has remained a community cornerstone, featuring a mix of blockbusters, film festival fare, and more obscure hidden gems, weathering many financial crises and even a brush with death in the late 1980s as the building was threatened with demolition. Through the efforts of locals and the dedicated staff, the theater has not only survived, but thrived, expanding its programming and renovating the historic space. In addition to movies, the Coolidge hosts numerous special events, hosting greats like Dennis Hopper and Norman Mailer, plus celebs, including Jakob Dylan and Julianne Moore.

The late-night program in particular, according to the Coolidge, focuses on the "horrifying, weird, camp, avant garde, tripped-out, and cult," so even buffs of the most bizarre movies might find themselves discovering a new favorite on 35mm film.

Address 290 Harvard Street, Brookline, MA 02446, +1 (617) 734-2501, www.coolidge.org |
Getting there Subway to Coolidge Corner (Green "C" Line) | Hours See website for
schedule | Tip While you're in the neighborhood, pay a visit to Boston General Store
(305 Harvard Street, Brookline, www.bostongeneralstore.com), which is chock-full of
home goods and sleek vintage accessories.

28_ Curio Spice Co.
A little goes a long way

Curio Spice Co. is a tiny shop that packs a wallop with the amount of flavor it has managed to stock along its small walls. It's a bit like stepping back into the times when traders went abroad and returned with parcels from which the stories of their journey wafted.

From this particular trader, you can buy singular spices, like dill pollen, wild Afghan cumin, pickled cherry blossoms, and over 20 varieties of pepper. But Curio is best known for its sublime spice mixes. A favorite of celebrity chef Bobby Flay's is "Kozani," which features fennel, lemon peel, bee pollen, lemon verbena, oregano, sage, and Greek saffron. Or "Da Lat," a Vietnamese-style spice rub featuring cocoa nibs, coffee, black pepper, star anise, ginger, coriander, turmeric, and cassia from the cinnamon family.

Curio stocks salts from places around the world, such as Cambodia and the Aegean Sea, and also from Martha's Vineyard and Maine right around the corner. The salts come in sweet flavors (vanilla salt, yuzu salt) and savory (seaweed salt, truffle salt). Best of all is something called "Magic Salt," which is so good that those who love it don't talk about it too much because they fear it will become too popular and not as readily available to them!

But definitely take the time to talk to folks here rather than trying to guess out how to use all of this exotic stuff in your own kitchen. Curio offers recipes for applying each spice mix; books for learning more about types of spices; grinders, graters, and other tools for using fresh spices; regular sampling/tasting events; and workshops for those who want to want to learn even more.

Curio was founded by Claire Cheney as a B-corporation, a category of business certified as having a positive social and environmental impact through its work. So you can also rest assured that your spices were sourced in a way that was as savory as their flavor.

Address 2265 Massachusetts Avenue, Cambridge, MA 02140, +1 (617) 945-1888, www.curiospice.com, support@curiospice.com | Getting there Subway to Davis (Red Line) | Hours Tue–Fri 11am–7pm, Sat & Sun 10am–6pm | Tip Why not pick up some music to cook by at Blue Bag Records, a vintage record store a few doors down (2325 Massachusetts Avenue, Cambridge, www.bluebagrecords.com)?

29 Cutler Majestic Theatre

Gilded playhouse with a long and spirited history

The Cutler Majestic Theatre is one of the most sumptuous places to see a performance in Boston, and it has been since the early 1900s. Its giant, vintage-inspired marquee is iconic of Boston's Theater District, and lines often snake around the block for its most popular events. The lavish Majestic was the second performance venue in the theater district, and the first theater in Boston to be wired for electricity, its domed interior aglow with over 4,500 light bulbs embedded among its many, many, many reliefs of fruit, flowers, leaves, masks and angels.

Nicknamed "the house of gold" for its over-the-top, Beaux Arts-style gilding and red velvet details, the Majestic was originally intended as an opera house. It has famously fabulous acoustics no matter where you sit. But the theater went through phases of various specialties from Vaudeville to film before being purchased by Emerson College in 1983. Restored to its full original glory for its 100th anniversary in 2003, the theater now looks exactly as it did when Isabella Stewart Gardner, Boston's most famous patron of the arts, sat down to watch the musical comedy *The Storks* on opening night in 1903. But the theater also has a dark side.

In addition to being a crown jewel of Boston architecture, The Cutler Majestic is rumored to be deeply haunted. Regularly sighted ghosts include a couple in Edwardian dress in the balcony who always leave before the second act; an elusive young girl who cries and asks for sweets; and former Boston mayor George A. Hibbard, whose wife took up acting (an activity unbefitting the widow of a politician at the time) in a production there shortly after his death. Seats are said to flip down and back up again without any visible inhabitants standing up or sitting down, and a backstage room known as "the nightmare room" has given several Emerson students panic attacks because of its inexplicably "oppressive energy."

Address 219 Tremont Street, Boston, MA 02116, +1 (617) 824-8400, www.cutlermajestic.org/online, tickets@emersontheatres.org | Getting there Subway to Boylston (Green Line), Park Street (Green or Red Line), or Tufts Medical Center (Orange Line) | Hours See website for schedule | Tip Want a little more occult action? Take a tour of the mosaic-encrusted Grand Lodge of Masons, the oldest Freemason headquarters in the US (186 Tremont Street, Boston, www.massfreemasonry.org/the-grand-lodge).

30 Darryl's Corner Bar

Probably the best soul food in Boston

One of the things Boston is not known for is its soul food. But there is one place where you can get heaping plates of steaming Southern comfort food in the middle of a brutal Boston winter, and that's Darryl's Corner Bar & Kitchen (DCBK) in the South End.

When the windows are steamed up on cold days, this is the kind of place where the steam is just as likely to be coming from the food as it is from a smoking jazz band or a crowd getting down to it. Following in the footsteps of Bob the Chef's Soul Food Temple, which inhabited the location for many years before Darryl's and hosted an infamous "all-you-can-eat Sunday Jazz and Gospel Brunch," DCBK has after-hours DJs and live jazz to accompany many weekend meals and to celebrate holidays like Valentine's Day and Martin Luther King Day. The unlimited buffet brunch on Sunday often turns into a dance party – if you can dance when you're that full.

And now it's time to tell you what will be filling your mouth, tummy, and senses: [Warning: The following is a list of menu items so tantalizing that reading on is going to make you salivate, and you'll be overrun with cravings until you actually get yourself to DCBK. So you may want to consider reading no further.] When you do reward yourself with a visit to DCBK, you can indulge in country fried chicken wings with sweet peach chili; Tennessee honey BBQ ribs; crispy cheddar polenta cakes and spinach succotash; lightly battered fried oysters with Cajun remoulade; braised beef short ribs with garlic mashed potatoes and green beans; and of course, smoky collard greens and candied yams. There are tasty vegetarian options, luscious cocktails and, of course, desserts – peach cobbler and whiskey cake! To a New Englander, walking through the door of Darryl's is like discovering another dimension. By the middle of February in Boston, it's a dimension you'll be eager to enter.

Address 604 Columbus Avenue, Roxbury, MA 02118, +1 (617) 536-1100, www.dcbkboston.com, info@dcbkboston.com | Getting there Subway to Massachusetts Avenue (Orange Line) | Hours Thu–Sat 4pm–midnight, Sun 10am–4pm | Tip Work off a big meal in Boston's beautiful Southwest Corridor Park, starting at the Butterfly Meadow and walking in either direction from there (Northampton Street and Southwest Corridor Path, Boston, www.swcpc.org).

31 Death of Quentin Compson

A tale of three plaques

In this city, we take our memorials very seriously, including those for completely fictional characters. Quentin Compson, a 19-year-old Harvard student who's featured in William Faulkner's *The Sound and The Fury* and *Absalom, Absalom!*, reached his demise in 1910 after jumping off the Anderson Memorial Bridge with tailor weights attached to his feet. His torment ran deep, a devastating combination of his family's tarnished reputation, his own guilty conscience, and general sense of culture shock after moving from Mississippi to Massachusetts (can you blame him?). The young man left a suicide note and a supposedly symbolic keepsake: his grandfather's broken pocket watch.

The community's dedication to the story throughout the years is truly commendable, since it involves not one, not two, but *three* different tributes. The first plaque was installed in 1965 by a Harvard graduate student and read: "Quentin Compson III. June 2, 1910. Drowned in the fading of honeysuckle." Unfortunately, it was accidentally removed during construction on the bridge in 1978, but its devotees didn't forget about it. By 1983, a replacement arrived, courtesy of a mystery benefactor, bearing a slightly different sentiment: "Drowned in the odour of honeysuckle," which was heavily debated and contested among local lit geeks for its reimagination of the text. The second edition made it all the way until 2014 before falling victim to yet another project on the bridge.

Fortunately, the third time's a charm, and the current plaque once again features the original text. Pro tip: the memorial is only the size of a single brick, so it's easy to miss and even more satisfying to find. In fact, locating it has become a rite of passage for new Harvard literature students keen to take on a scavenger hunt.

Address Anderson Memorial Bridge, Allston, MA 02134 | Getting there Subway to Harvard (Red Line) | Hours Unrestricted | Tip Make it a perfectly literary day with a visit to Longfellow House (105 Brattle Street, Cambridge, www.nps.gov/long/index.htm), a beautiful Georgian mansion built in 1759 that was home to the poet Henry Wadsworth Longfellow.

32 Dorchester Art Project

A creative space for art, music, and consciousness

Dorchester Art Project (DAP), a 5,000-square-foot art space sited in the historic Howard Building, is one of many eclectic endeavors by the scrappy non-profit Brain Arts Organization. Like Brain Arts itself, DAP is several entities in one.

It's a studio space for over a dozen local artists, many of them from the neighborhood and/or artists of color. It's also a music venue, devoting one small room (plus a dressing room for performers) to nightly live events that are often for all ages and feature a combination of local and national acts and almost every music genre you can imagine. And DAP is an art gallery, with two large spaces dedicated to showing cutting-edge, experimental artwork, including group and solo shows. The space has only been open for a few years now, and there has been an emphasis on multicultural perspectives, queer visions, and surreal or magical experiences. The shows, both musical and visual, tend to have a community-building undercurrent and frequently feature special programming associated with political events or themes. They are not like anything else happening in Boston. Openings are packed.

DAP also has a fabulous circulating 'zine library, featuring 'zines about art, music, literature, politics, feminism, activism, comics, and much more – many produced by artists from New England. The library accepts donations if you make 'zines or have a collection of 'zines you no longer need. There are regular open calls to participate in pop-up shows if you are any other kind of artist.

Brain Arts holds events all over Boston, but this building itself, their home base, is unique and cozy. The wallpaper is handmade (and trippy), the hallways are lined with flyers and art for sale, and the environment, staffed entirely by volunteers, is welcoming to anyone and everyone. The venue is available for rent for private performances, exhibitions, and workshops. Dorchester residents may receive special discounts.

Address 1486 Dorchester Avenue, Dorchester, MA 02122, www.dorchesterartproject.org, dorchesterartproject@gmail.com | **Getting there** Subway to Fields Corner (Red Line) | **Hours** See website for event schedule | **Tip** Dorchester has a large Vietnamese population and therefore some really delicious Vietnamese food. Go get Pho'd up before or after a show at DAP at local favorite Phở 2000 (198 Adams Street, Dorchester).

33 The Dutch House

A former hub of hot chocolate

While many of the homes in the tony suburb of Brookline look quite stately and elegant, there's one that truly seems of a completely different time and place. And that's because, well, it actually is. Built in Chicago for the 1893 World's Fair, the building was designed by the Amsterdam-based Van Houten Cocoa Company as a grand replica of the Franeker Town Hall in Friesland. Its coral and gray exterior boasts stepped gables and a mansard roof, windows with shimmering leaded green glass, and an ornate door frame that features a variety of stone animals inspired by the Enkhuizen Orphanage in the Netherlands.

The house was more than a façade. At the fair, it provided visitors with an entire experience that included pieces of Dutch décor and art, plus women in traditional garb serving hot cocoa samples to guests. One of those guests was Brookline's own Captain Charles Brooks Appleton. He was so enchanted with the house that he had it broken down, brick by brick, shipped from Chicago to Massachusetts, and reconstructed on Netherlands Road. And, yes, the street was named after the home, presumably because it was so striking.

Today, the home is a private, multi-unit, residential building and one of just a handful of surviving structures from the 1893 World's Fair. After some of the exterior elements deteriorated, sculptor Beckie Kravitz was commissioned to restore them to their former glory in recent years, using old photographs. These touches included friezes, corbel caps, panels, and castings.

The interior retains the majority of the original character and quirks, including 300-year-old, blue and white Delftware tiles, Flemish wood paneling, grand fireplaces, and high ceilings. If you want to take a peek for yourself without waiting for an apartment to open up, the home's online listings are full of jaw-dropping photos that will give you a little glimpse into its glorious past.

Address 20 Netherlands Road, Brookline, MA 02445 | Getting there Subway to Mission Park (Green "E" Line) | Hours Unrestricted from the outside only | Tip On a chilly day, bring your own cup of cocoa to savor as you wander over to quaint Linden Park nearby (Linden Street, Brookline).

34 E. E. Cummings' Grave
The last stanza

Ironically, the headstone of the poet best known for bucking the accepted rules of capitalization in his work bears his full and proper name: Edward Estlin Cummings. Even more perplexing, the man who dedicated his life to the beauty of words has no epitaph. Though Cummings passed away at age 67 in North Conway, New Hampshire from a stroke on September 3, 1962, his final resting place is in Jamaica Plain's Forest Hills Cemetery. Buried next to the poet is his third wife, Marion Morehouse, a model and photographer.

Cummings was born in Cambridge in 1894 and began writing poetry at the ripe old age of eight. He attended Harvard for both his undergraduate and graduate degrees. After working for a short time after graduation as a book dealer, he took a detour to serve as an ambulance corps volunteer during World War I in France. It was during this period that he was arrested for treason due to his vocal anti-war stance. Contrary to popular belief, it was a long road to success for Cummings, and it wasn't until his 50s and 60s that he began to achieve widespread acclaim for his work.

Visitors often leave notes with their own handwritten verses on the gravestone, along with coins and flowers. The tributes don't end here, however. Just a short walk away is a small, cozy structure created by artist Mitch Ryerson in 2002 called *The Opening*. Carved from a sugar maple tree, decorated with a copper roof, and topped with a bird, the hideaway is completely dedicated to the poet, featuring one of his poems stamped into the bronze floor and a book of his work, along with a sitting area designed for losing yourself in his verses. A popular site for contemplation, the space provides a tangible symbol of both thoughtful reflection and transformation. According to Ryerson's statement about the work, he likes "the idea of experiencing an e e cummings poem as an event."

Address 95 Forest Hills Avenue, Jamaica Plain, MA 02130, +1 (617) 524-0128, www.foresthillscemetery.com | **Getting there** Subway to Forest Hills (Orange Line). On Althea Path in the cemetery, Cummings' grave is to the left of the CLARKE headstone, flush to the ground. | **Hours** Daily 8am–4:30pm | **Tip** Head up to Cambridge to see Cummings' birthplace (104 Irving Street, Cambridge), which is now a residential building.

35 Echo Bridge
Hear, hear

Practice your best "Ricola!" yodel before stepping onto the platform underneath this beautiful masonry arch, which was built in 1877 by Boston Water Works. True to its namesake, you'll hear up to 15 reverberations back after they ring out across the banks of the Charles River.

Though no one can definitively pinpoint the reason for this phenomenon, there are a few pretty plausible theories. The most popular explanation is that the echoes are the result of the sound bouncing between the bridge and the water, though it's also been suggested that the noise is funneled through the bridge's arc, similar to the effect that can be observed in the arches at Manhattan's Grand Central Terminal. Others, like Arthur Taber Jones, believe that it might be a combination of the two. In his study conducted for the *Journal of the Acoustical Society of America,* he sought to get to the bottom of it with mixed results, literally, as both ideas seemed to be true. No matter what's behind it, one thing is for certain: there's nothing else like it around. Musicians have even been known to set up shop on the platform and have jam sessions to take advantage of the excellent acoustics and marvel at an anomaly that's just plain cool.

In addition to the amazing sonic spectacle, the bridge is a visual beauty to behold, spanning 500 feet between the towns of Needham and Newton. There are seven arches in all, along with postcard-perfect views of the Hemlock Gorge, a waterfall, and old mill buildings in the distance. Within the Gorge, there are a number of walking trails ideal for getting lost on a Sunday afternoon. Keep your eyes peeled for the ruins of a 19th-century mill that was once powered by the river.

The bridge is a part of the Sudbury Aqueduct and connects Framingham's Sudbury Reservoir and the Chestnut Hill Reservoir. While it once carried water throughout the Boston metro area, the aqueduct hasn't been functional since the 1950s.

Address Ellis Street, Newton, MA 02464 | **Getting there** Subway to Eliot (Green "D" Line) | **Hours** Unrestricted | **Tip** Produce even more beautiful sounds with the violins, cellos, and upright basses at Johnson String Instrument (1029 Chestnut Street, Newton Upper Falls, www.johnsonstring.com), which has been pluckin' away since 1976.

36_ Edes & Gill

Time travel to a colonial printing shop

In 1764, on the eve of the American Revolutionary War, journalist and political agitator Benjamin Edes and printer John Gill began publishing *The Boston Gazette* and *The Country Journal*. This is no coincidence. The papers served to fan the flames of revolution, acting as the public voice of a group, led by Samuel Adams, known as the Boston Radicals. Adams' radical idea was to form a union of the colonies and collectively secede from Great Britain. In 1773, Edes, a man of words and action, was one of the founding members of the group who, dressed as American Indians, snuck down to Boston Harbor's Griffin's Wharf and dumped boxes of British tea over the sides of three ships moored there: the *Beaver*, the *Dartmouth*, and the *Eleanor*.

When the British stormed Boston two years later, Edes fled by boat along the Charles River, carrying a printing press with him, and ultimately re-established the press in Watertown. Gill was not so lucky. He sat in jail in Boston, charged with treason and sedition.

Though it's not using the same press that Edes fled with in 1775, The Printing Office of Edes & Gill reopened its doors in 2011, looking and operating much as it did back then. It continues to do exactly the work it was doing in the 1770s. This historically accurate re-creation of the original Edes & Gill print shop pays homage to these historical activists and the importance of journalism. They also give live demonstrations – while wearing full period costumes – of colonial printing processes. It's an inky, hands on, immersive experience suited for history buffs of all ages. The press is also actively producing replicas of historical documents, including the United States Constitution, samples of which can be taken home by visitors.

A visit here is a quirky way to get a visceral sense of how the accretive actions of regular people snowballed into the creation of a whole new nation-state and political system.

Address 1 Faneuil Hall Square, Boston, MA 02109, www.bostongazette.org | Getting there Subway to Government Center (Blue or Green Line) or to State (Orange or Blue Line) | Hours Mon–Sat 10am–9pm, Sun 10am–6pm | Tip Gary Gregory, Founder and Print Master at Edes and Gill, also runs Lessons on Liberty at the Boston Commons Visitor Center (139 Tremont Street, Boston, www.lessonsonliberty.com), a small company that gives fascinating walking tours of historically significant parts of Boston.

37 — Esh Circus Arts

Join the circus for a few hours or forever

Short of maybe fireworks, there is really nothing as spectacular as watching an aerial artist at work. The combination of strength, grace, and gravity involved in acrobatic choreography occurring high above your head will always take your breath away, no matter how many times you see it. It's so incredible to watch that it's hard to imagine *you* could ever walk across a tightrope, twirl yourself down from the sky on a silk ribbon, leap from one swinging bar to another, or hang by one knee from a hoop. But you can! These beautiful things can be learned, even if you are out of shape, afraid of heights, and believe yourself to be congenitally clumsy.

5,000 square-foot Esh Circus Arts in Somerville caters to professionals and beginners alike with equal encouragement and enthusiasm. There are classes for overall fitness but with a twist – or perhaps a tumble – using the playfulness and unique perspective that circus experts bring to general working out.

Hardcore developmental training is available as well for those who are seriously considering going pro. There are also classes for clowning, juggling, and hula hooping, if you're just looking to improve your hand-eye coordination, shake your life up a little, or vastly diversify your life skills. Esh also teaches circus arts to children. So if your young ones are bendy, clowny, or just need to burn off energy, they can literally bounce off of the walls here. They can also train intensively to run away with the circus.

All of Esh's classes are small, with five students per teacher. All 30 of their teaching staff are experts in their specialties, and many trained at the highly acclaimed New England Center for Circus Arts. Esh also holds occasional intimate touring circus performances in their unique Somerville studio, and they can also host circus-filled birthday parties should you ever desire one.

Address 44 Park Street, Somerville, MA 02143, +1 (617) 764-0190, www.eshcircusarts.com, info@eshcircusarts.com | **Getting there** Subway to Porter (Red Line); bus 83 to Park Street & Beacon Street, bus 86 to Washington Street & Beacon Street, or bus 87 to Somerville Avenue & Central Street | **Hours** See website for classes and events | **Tip** Tumble on over to the Somerville Museum (1 Westwood Road, Somerville, www.somervillemuseum.org), featuring constantly changing exhibitions about Somerville's current and historical cultural, ecological, and artistic activities.

38 Ether Monument

An homage to the comfortably numb

If you're looking for a peaceful and picturesque place to picnic, try one of the benches surrounding this elegant statue and fountain in Boston's Public Garden. When you pause here, you may find the delicately splashing fountain and intricately carved granite figure tenderly washing the breast of another are especially soothing, and there's a reason for it: the monument celebrates the first use of anesthesia in surgery to bring about "insensibility to pain."

In the 1840s, a young dentist named William Thomas Green Morton was struggling to convince patients who needed their teeth extracted that the long-term benefits of the surgery were worth the short-term pain. They believed him up to a point – the point when he actually began to extract their teeth – and then immediately ceased to believe. So Morton went about trying to determine a way to remove pain temporarily from the equation, experimenting with everything from brandy (not strong enough) to laudanum (waaay too strong!).

Inspired by a predecessor in this line of inquiry, a dentist in Connecticut named Horace Wells, and heartened by a few successful experiences getting his dog high on ether, Morton tried the gas on a human and concluded that it would work. He was so confident that he told a friend, "I shall have my patients coming in at one door, have all their teeth extracted without knowing it, and then, going into the next room to have a full set put in." In 1846, Morton demonstrated the technique to spectators at Massachusetts General Hospital in what has since been known as the "Ether Dome," successfully removing a tumor from a local printer's jaw without the patient experiencing any pain.

The monument was gifted to the city in 1868 by retired merchant Thomas Lee, who had especially strong feelings of "gratitude for the relief of human suffering occasioned by the discovery of the anesthetic properties of sulphuric ether."

Address Boston Public Garden near the intersection of Arlington and Marlborough Streets, Boston, MA 02116, +1 (617) 635-4505, www.cityofboston.gov/parks | **Getting there** Subway to Arlington (Green Line), use Commonwealth Avenue entrance to the garden | **Hours** Daily dawn–dusk | **Tip** Go full tourist and grab a beer at the bar that inspired the 1980s television show *Cheers*, right around the corner from the Ether Monument (84 Beacon Street, Boston, www.cheersboston.com/locations/beacon).

39 Fake Viking Memorials
Remembering what never was

In the 1870s, some wealthy and powerful people in the Boston area were collectively struck with Viking fever. The origin of this strange disease seems to be a Viking-obsessed popular musician who went by the moniker "Ole Bull," which should have been a tip off that he might not be totally on the up and up. Ole Bull, whose real name at birth was "Ole Bornemann Bull" was a classical violinist, originally from Norway. He was a Norwegian nationalist at the time when Norway was working on becoming independent from Sweden. And he was a firm believer in an unsubstantiated theory, set forth by Danish scholar Carl Christian Rafn, that the legendary "Vinland" of the Viking sagas was actually New England.

Bull stayed with the venerable Henry Wadsworth Longfellow while visiting Boston and managed to convince him and over 50 other prominent Boston citizens (including the president of Harvard at the time) that the city needed to raise funds and erect a sculptural tribute to Norse explorer Leif Eriksson. The basic theory was that around 1000 AD, Eriksson traveled across New England (known as "Norumbega" in Norwegian lore), sailed up the Charles River, and lived for a time in Cambridge. Another major proponent of this theory was Eben Norton Horsford, Harvard professor of chemistry, amateur archeologist, and baking soda magnate due to his ability to apply chemistry-based principles to industry. He helped underwrite much of the Massachusetts memorabilia associated with this Norse mythology.

There are markers of this false history all the way up into Maine, but in Boston, you can find a statue of Leif Eriksson on the Commonwealth Avenue Mall, a plaque in Cambridge where his house supposedly once stood, and many Norse designs carved into bridges along the Charles River that celebrate this completely fabricated story. Horsford also built a tower in Weston, MA honoring Norumbega.

Address Statue is in the Commonwealth Avenue Mall near the intersection of Commonwealth and Charlesgate Avenues. Marker is along Memorial Drive's Gerry's Landing Road at Greenough Boulevard. | **Getting there** Subway to Hynes Convention Center (Green "B", "C", or "D" Lines) for statue; subway to Harvard (Red Line) for plaque | **Hours** Unrestricted | **Tip** Visit Berkley, MA to see the possible Viking markings on Dighton Rock and a small museum devoted to several strange theories associated with them (3rd Avenue, Berkeley, www.mass.gov/locations/dighton-rock-state-park).

40_ Fat Baby

And the cutest crapper award goes to…

Fat Baby, a hip sushi bar and cocktail lounge in South Boston, also has one of the cutest bathroom concepts ever: fat babies. It's like the internet in there nine months after a blizzard. Every employee's chubby cheeks have made it to the bathroom wall, along with some cheeks belonging to a few local and visiting celebrities.

Part of the charm of this nouveau pan-Asian restaurant, helmed by folks who have been cooking, bartending, and managing restaurants in South Boston and along the waterfront for a decade or more, is that it grew out of relationships with regular diners and drinkers from the neighborhood. The owner was invited by a regular at another of his South Boston restaurants, Loco Taqueria & Oyster Bar, to go on a Southeast Asian trip that exposed him to a whole range of cuisine and subtle flavors he'd not had contact with before. Inspired by the trip, and with tons of encouragement from regulars at his other restaurants, Fat Baby's concept became a reality just a few blocks away from Loco.

Originally, "fat baby" was a code name that the team had for the space as they were building it out because it was their smallest but widest restaurant. Now, the space is more "sleek adult" with geisha murals by local artist Mark Grundig, exposed brick walls, and warm wood paneling. But the fat baby theme has exploded into the bathroom, where hundreds of baby pictures (keep an eye out for fat baby Jay-Z among other celebrities) overwhelm you with so much cuteness you may forget you had to pee.

If it takes more than a baby-filled bathroom to get you to South Boston, consider visiting Fat Baby on one of their special dining deal days such as Dollar Dumpling Night or Maki Mondays, or check their social media feeds for sushi-making classes. Then, once you're there, grab a Fat Baby "Miso Cute" t-shirt and head straight to the john to take infant-infused selfies.

Address 118 Dorchester Street, South Boston, MA 02127, +1 (617) 766-3450, www.fatbabysouthboston.com | **Getting there** Subway to Andrew (Red Line) | **Hours** Mon–Fri 4pm–midnight, Sat & Sun 11am–midnight | **Tip** Do some off-the-beaten-path, high-end thrifting before your sushi at Covet (391 West Broadway, South Boston, www.covetboston.com).

41 Fenway Park Living Museum

Behind the batting cages

Boston is a sports town. Not just a sports town, actually, but more like A SPORTS TOWN! This isn't something that can be explained in words, even in all caps. It's something that you can only understand by riding a Green Line train through Kenmore Square before or after a Red Sox game. Boston loves its football and basketball teams too. But the Red Sox, and even more so, Fenway Park, the team's home field, is so essentially a part of Boston's DNA that even those of you who don't see any value in sports should take an afternoon pilgrimage to the field just once to see "The Green Monster," its over-37-foot left field wall, with your own eyes. Otherwise, you run the risk of being thrown out of the city for lack of proper reverence.

Those of you who do care deeply about sports should go well beyond that and visit The Fenway Park Living Museum. This museum, only accessible through Fenway Park tours, treats Red Sox superfans to more than 170,000 pieces of memorabilia related to the team dating all the way back to the 1930s. Among the can't-miss artifacts: 36 baseball bats used in World Series games, 90 team-signed World Series baseballs, and the lockers of Ted Williams and Johnny Pesky.

It's not the historic news clippings or well-worn sporting equipment, but the intimacy of the experience that makes the museum so special. Wending your way through the bowels of Fenway Park, you'll hear echoes of every cheer and razz, inhale the scent of hotdogs and popcorn, and pass through the same entrances as all the players who have made their way onto the field for thousands of games. You'll get access to behind-the-scenes dirt, but you'll also get a visceral experience of all of the ecstatic wins and dismal losses where they occurred. And it's all so good.

Address Fenway Park, 4 Jersey Street, Boston, MA 02215, +1 (617) 226-6666, www.mlb.com/redsox/ballpark/museum | Getting there Subway to Kenmore (Green "B," "C," or "D" Lines) | Hours See website for seasonal hours; call to schedule tour | Tip If your visit aligns with a game day, Autograph Alley (at the Jersey Street Team Store for now, but it moves around) hosts a former Boston Red Sox player, coach, or personality before each home game to sign autographs free of charge (108 Brookline Avenue, Boston, www.jerseystreetstore.com).

42 Films at the Gate

Open-air Kung Fu movies with takeout

Every summer, Boston's Chinatown hosts free outdoor movie screen-ings right next to the Chinatown Gate, the neighborhood's main entrance. There are several outdoor summer screening series in Bos-ton, but this one has a special vibe to it. Rather than popcorn, mov-ie-goers get Asian takeout from local restaurants and then gather, old and young alike, on donated and brought-from-home folding chairs and watch a curated series of films in Chinese (sometimes Cantonese, sometimes Mandarin) with English subtitles. The films range from features to documentaries, all set in Asian communities or countries. Every season includes at least one classic Kung Fu film.

It's a decidedly urban experience. The screenings are right along-side an entrance to the turnpike, so cars and trucks blow by at high speed and honk at one another while filmgoers jeer aloud at foolish characters and pass cardboard take out boxes back and forth among themselves. But the whole experience is very communal – the oppo-site of watching a movie in a dark theater or on your personal blanket at a public park. Funky food smells surround you. People walking along Chinatown's main drag stop and stand between old-school metal-folding chair "rows" to watch for a while before moving on.

The Kung Fu nights get the biggest crowds, and it's not uncom-mon to have kids racing around re-enacting well-known fight scenes. You are expected to wince and cheer at well-landed blows and to clap at happy endings. Unless they're sappy. Groan for those.

The non-Kung Fu films are usually classics or lesser known, for-eign or independent, many getting their only screening in the Boston area here – and definitely not films you'll find on Netflix. So bring some friends and try out some food from a Chinatown restaurant you've never been to before. Get a good grip on your chopsticks, soak in the unique environment, and enjoy the show!

Address Vacant lot on Hudson Street between Beach & Kneeland Streets, or in
Chinatown Park on the Rose Fitzgerald Kennedy Greenway, www.filmsatthegate.org,
info@filmsatthegate.org | Getting there Subway to Chinatown (Orange Line),
South Station (Red Line), or Boylston (Green Line) | Hours See website for schedule |
Tip The Coolidge Corner Theater's "Coolidge at the Greenway" series is programmed
by the theater's curators and projected (always!) in 35mm (Rose Kennedy Greenway,
Atlantic Avenue, Boston, www.coolidge.org/programs/coolidge-greenway).

43 The First Casualty
The Revolutionary War takes its first life

There's some debate about who was the first American to be killed in the Revolutionary War. In 1770, the colonies of Massachusetts struggled with their intertwined desires for highly taxed – but also higher quality – British goods, and their independence. Boston was officially boycotting and pushing other colonies to join them, but after a few years, merchants gave in and began paying the exorbitant import taxes. Tempers around these issues ran high, and the newspapers of the day fanned the flames.

Shopkeeper Theophilus Lillie publicly announced his plans to break the boycott, arguing that those fighting for freedom were hypocrites for pressuring him to conform to it. Christopher Seider, son of German immigrants and part of a group of several young "working boys" in tune with the tensions of the time, taunted Lillie outside his home, calling him an "importer." It quickly turned into real protest.

A loyalist customs officer Ebenezer Richardson tried to disperse the crowd, but people chased him home. Through his window, he fired "swan pellets" with a musket into the crowd, hitting Christopher Seider, who died by the end of the day on February 22, 1770. The incident is seen by many as the moment that instigated the Boston Massacre.

Others count the Boston Massacre itself about a week and half later as the official beginning of the Revolutionary War. They argue that Crispus Attucks, a Native- and African-American patriot shot twice in the chest by British soldiers during the famous confrontation, should be identified, as Stevie Wonder famously puts it in his song *Black Man*, as "The first man to die for the flag we now hold high."

The final resting place for both men is a shared gravesite in Boston's Granary Burying Ground, not far from the eternal homes of some of the country's most famous revolutionaries: Paul Revere, Samuel Adams, and John Hancock.

Address 95 Tremont Street, Boston, MA 02108, www.boston.gov/cemeteries/granary-burying-ground, parks@boston.gov | Getting there Subway to Park Street (Red or Green Line). Inside the cemetery gate, turn right to find the grave to the left of Samuel Adams' grave. | Hours Daily 9am–4pm | Tip If you want a deeper connection with the dead, book some time with a medium at Tremont Tea Room, the oldest psychic establishment in the country (333 Washington Street, Suite 207b, Boston, www.tremont-tearoom.com).

44 First Same-Sex Wedding

I do, you do, they do, we all do – since 2004!

Cambridge's City Hall building is architecturally significant in that it's designed by the famous architectural firm Longfellow, Alden & Harlow, in the Richardsonian Romanesque style. And built of an extremely ancient type of granite only found in Milford Massachusetts. But that's not why it will go down in history.

It will be remembered because this is the first place in the United States to issue a same-sex marriage license, and where, very soon after, the first state-sanctioned, same-sex marriage was performed.

Exactly 180 days after the Massachusetts Supreme Court Judicial upheld judgment in Goodridge v. Department of Public Health, this first license, issued to Marcia Hams and Susan Shepherd, was produced at 12:01am on May 17, 2004. And even though it was after midnight, there was a party. The city hall's main staircase was lavishly decorated with white organza, and thousands of people, many dressed to the nines of course, filled the front lawn of the building and street out front. Onlookers cheered on same-sex marriage license applicants as the long line of couples began flowing into the building. Live music, cake, and champagne toasts kept the festive atmosphere going into the wee hours of the morning.

Marriage licenses usually take three days to clear in Massachusetts, but the waiting period was waived in these cases as most couples applying had already been living together for decades. The first couple to wed, at 9:15am during the city's normal business hours, were Tanya McCloskey and Marcia Kadish. And then the city of Cambridge, and all of the other cities in Massachusetts were marrying same-sex couples for the rest of that day and since!

When gay marriage became legal in all 50 states in 2015, Cambridge City Hall rose to the occasion again, hosting a dance party on its front stoop for 25,000+ people.

Address 795 Massachusetts Avenue, Cambridge, MA 02139, +1 (617) 349-4000, www.cambridgema.gov/Services/applyforamarriagelicense | **Getting there** Subway to Central (Red Line) | **Hours** Mon 8:30am–8pm, Tue–Thu 8:30am–5pm, Fri 8:30am–noon | **Tip** Sadly, Cambridge's last (and most infamous) gay club, Paradise, closed in 2018, but you can still party pretty queer at Heroes, the long-standing, roving dance night (www.facebook.com/HEROES-58011712778).

45_Float

Get away from it all – literally

We all get overwhelmed from time to time. Our workload and personal responsibilities leave us feeling like we're about to blow a circuit. In an ideal world, we'd go on vacation. But that's not always possible. What is always possible, however, is floating.

Floating, for the uninitiated, is like taking a bath, except the "bath" is super, super salty, and the "tub" is more of a space pod. You don't so much submerge yourself, as hover in it. Like a bath, a float is deeply relaxing, but you don't lock the bathroom door, light scented candles, and sink up to your chin in hot water and foamy bubbles when you float. Rather, you shut off all sensory input, relieving yourself of gravity, light, sound, a sense of temperature difference between your body and everything else that exists – and simply *be*. You're almost in a womb-like state for about an hour. If it sounds like doing nothing, it is. That's the beauty of it. It's very hard for us to stop, *really* turn our brains off, and take a break from everything, and flotation tanks do that for us instantly. Just close the tank, settle in, and enjoy all the nothing. Tons and tons of nothing to float within – until your time is up, and you must emerge.

Float's bright little space brings floating, originally reserved for athletes and meditation experts, to the common people – people who shoveled their cars out of parking spots in a blizzard, or waited for an MBTA bus longer than they should have just to get here and float. The price is accessible, with special rates for teachers, artists, and first responders, and newbies will feel entirely safe and welcome.

The touted benefits of floating include relieving pain from arthritis, back pain, muscle pain, fibromyalgia, and alleviating psychological distress from stress, depression, anxiety, and PTSD. You may also have a more metaphysical experience, like increased mindfulness, improved self-awareness, or that elusive, oneness-with-the-universe feeling.

Address 515 Medford Street, Somerville, MA 02145, +1 (844) 443-5628, www.floatboston.com, info@floatboston.com | Getting there Bus 89 to Broadway & Medford Street (Magoun Square) | Hours Wed–Mon 7am–9:15pm, Tue 3–9:15pm | Tip After your mind has been opened wide by floating, go fill it with some wild contemporary art at Tufts University's Art Galleries, about a 20-minute walk up Broadway (40 Talbot Avenue, Medford, artgalleries.tufts.edu).

46 Formaggio Kitchen
Spelunking for Stilton

If there's a secret to happiness, it probably involves one of the three Cs: cheese, chocolate, and charcuterie. Fortunately, Cambridge's Formaggio Kitchen has an abundance of each, plus all the homemade baked goods, wine, and olives your discerning heart desires. The shelves of this gourmet grocer are stocked with specialty foods and gift baskets designed to be the highlight of any dinner party.

Since 1978, Formaggio has thoughtfully sourced their artisanal cheeses directly from producers to make sure it maintains an exceptional selection. "Owners Ihsan and Valerie Gurdal were inspired by the French tradition of *affinage* in France, a profession devoted to storing and maturing cheese for sale," says assistant general manager Liz Moroney. "To store cheese at the optimal temperature and humidity, Formaggio Kitchen became the first American retail shop to have its own aging cave."

Every day, you can marvel at the global flavors of the store's cheese counter. It's cleverly displayed as a world map, so sampling specialties from different countries is almost as good as an international vacation. "We stay true to the tradition of cheesemongering," Moroney explains. "Our personalized customer service through guided tasting is a way to learn about cheese and find the perfect one for your occasion."

Whether you're an aspiring cheese snob or just looking to sharpen your knowledge of manchego and mozzarella, drop into one of the store's "Cheese 101" or "Chocolate, Wine, and Cheese" classes. Or delve into the depths of the stinky cheese underground with a "Brave the Caves" event. As summer rolls around, the staff take to the streets to celebrate by grilling massive quantities of smoked meats at their Saturday afternoon barbeques. While this location is the original and most beloved, you can also get your *fromage* fix at outposts in Kendall Square and the South End.

Address 360 Huron Avenue, Cambridge, MA 02138, +1 (617) 354-4750,
www.formaggiokitchen.com, contactus@formaggiokitchen.com | Getting there Subway to
Alewife, Porter, or Harvard (Red Line); bus 75 to Huron Avenue & Chilton Street,
bus 74 or 78 to Concord Avenue & Huron Avenue | Hours Mon–Fri 9am–7pm,
Sat 9am–6pm, Sun 10am–4pm | Tip Once you've planned out your fancy food menu,
spruce up your digs before company arrives with some vintage, mid-century modern
furniture from Reside (266 Concord Avenue, Cambridge, www.resideinc.com).

47 Franklin Park Bear Pens
A grisly grizzly relic

We've all been there. You start a project with the highest of hopes, and it doesn't work out so well. But rather than go through the tedium of dismantling it, you just walk away instead. The almost-forgotten bear pens at Franklin Park Zoo are proof that it happens to the best of us. The zoo was incredibly successful during its heyday in the early 20th century. Each of the open-air cages housed a different species of bear, from grizzly to polar, that strutted around to the delight of visitors at the completely free attraction. However, all good things must come to an end, and changes at the zoo led to the permanent shutdown of the exhibit in 1954.

While plans to tear down the pens were made more than once, people just never got around to it, presumably moving on to bigger and better animal enclosures. The result is a slightly sad, slightly haunting, and extremely large set of metal and stone cages that sit in Long Crouch Woods on the outskirts of the park, wasting away. Further complicating the situation is the fact that it's still unclear who actually owns the pens. The zoo wasn't originally under the jurisdiction of the city, and there's never been a formal agreement between the two entities beyond a verbal contract. So there they stay, untouched, bare, and totally bearless, a bizarre memorial of sorts to the site's former grandeur.

If this spot looks eerily familiar, that's likely because it scored some time on the silver screen as the location of a murder victim in 2003's *Mystic River*. Indeed, the deterioration has given the cages almost menacing quality, with rusted roofing and metal spikes dangling threateningly and haphazardly throughout the structures. One striking piece of the past that has remained intact and can still be spotted on the back of one of the pens is the gorgeous, stately engraving of two bears holding up the 1912 Boston seal.

Address Franklin Park Road, Roxbury, MA 02121, +1 (617) 635-4505, www.boston.gov/
parks/franklin-park | Getting there Subway to Stony Brook (Orange Line). In the park,
climb the hill north of White Stadium. | Hours Daily dawn–dusk | Tip While you're in
Franklin Park, why not go straight to the source? Architect Frederick Law Olmsted's former
home and design office is a short drive away (99 Warren Street, Brookline, www.nps.gov/frla).

48 Friend Smithsonian Museum

A wee bit of art

It might be a very, very small fraction of the size of the actual Smithsonian in Washington, DC, but the tiny museum in front of Martha Friend's Somerville home is actually one of the best places to view unique work from local artists. By tiny, we're talking 24" high by 36" wide and 30" deep. But this petite corner of culture is weather-proof and illuminated, and admission is free. Think of it as a Little Free Library, but filled with rotating works of art. It features new exhibits from different creators from the area every single month.

An artist and former professional photographer herself, Friend loves repurposing found objects and turning them into beautiful pieces. She established this Smithsonian as an alternative to the traditional concept of a brick-and-mortar museum and all of the limitations that tend to come along with it. "I was reminded of how important it is to have art everywhere, and free, and in unexpected places like someone's front yard," she explains. "Why not a tiny museum with changing exhibits that's open and accessible 24 hours a day? The exhibits vary, from art by kids to work by established artists."

"It's most successful when someone discovers it accidentally," she says. Past exhibits have included a steampunk-inspired forest made of recycled metal, a menagerie of handmade animals, and watercolor paintings. Part of the charm and allure is its novelty.

But wait, there's more! As a bonus, there's currently an outdoor installation of the *Wizard of Oz*'s Emerald City on display, which Friend built in 2015 for fun. Fans of the classic film will appreciate the yellow brick road and the creative reimagination of Dorothy's promised land. "It's made of green glass of all kinds and stands 10 feet tall. People absolutely love it, and it makes them happy," she gushes.

Address 135 Highland Avenue, Somerville, MA 02143, www.marthafriend.com/mf_
friendsmith.php, marthafriend@gmail.com | **Getting there** Bus 88 or 90 to 125 Highland
Avenue | **Hours** Daily 11am – dusk | **Tip** Attend a poetry reading, an in-the-round musical jam
session, or a craft market at the Center for Arts at the Armory (191 Highland Avenue, No. 1C,
Somerville, www.artsatthearmory.org), a community staple in a repurposed militia building.

49__Garden of Peace

A living tribute to Boston murder victims

It's hard to think about death, and it's even harder to think about homicide. But it happens, and it happens to real people. When it does, their friends and families need ways to heal. The Garden of Peace is both an antidote to the horror of lives cut short, and a living reminder of them collectively and as individuals.

This quiet oasis for reflection, tucked behind the statehouse in bustling downtown Boston, was organized by local women activists whose families had been impacted by homicide. The garden has been designed to function as "a journey from grief to renewal," and has over a dozen features towards this end including symbolic plantings, walkways intended to help keep people grounded in the present, seating areas for private introspection, sculptures, and water features.

Central to the garden is a winding stone "stream" and stone benches, all carved with the names and dates of birth and death of murdered Bostonians. The names are touchstones where families return to and reminisce, but they are also a way for everyone else to see murder victims as very specific, real people. Many of the stories told in the briefest possible way in stone – simply a name and pair of dates – are told in more detail on the garden's website, should you want to learn about gentle, guitar strumming, 18-year old Gabe Bardo, murdered over a tiny bag of marijuana in 2017. Or Suzanne Rudin, who made jewelry and demoed and remodeled her home before becoming a victim of domestic violence in 2018. Or Christian Rosa who loved fishing, boating, and his daughter Mekeya, and who was gunned down at age 21 while retrieving some dry cleaning.

It might be a stretch to call the Garden of Peace anyone's "happy place," but it's a lovely place to be thoughtful and calm. It's a real retreat for anyone living with a sharp sense of loss and in need of an inspiring place to sit with those feelings.

Address 64–98 Somerset Street, Boston, MA 02108, +1 (617) 586-1369, www.mass.gov/orgs/garden-of-peace, gardenofpeace@mass.gov | **Getting there** Subway to Government Center (Green Line), Bowdoin (Blue Line), or Park Street (Red or Green Line) | **Hours** Daily dawn–dusk | **Tip** At the exit from Government Center is one of the most famous examples of Brutalist architecture in the world, Boston's City Hall. Exhibitions inside feature Boston artists (1 City Hall Square, Boston, www.boston.gov).

50 The Garment District

Not your grandma's store – but maybe her jeans!

The Garment District bills itself as a "department store," but this is a bit misleading, as it's likely the only store in the world whose departments include "Cowboy Boots," "New Wave, Grunge & More," and "Ties and Suspenders."

This eclectic, multi-level building full of clothing and accessories is most famous for two things: its costumes (as in Halloween, but all year long) and its early morning "by-the-pound" sales. The costumes are among the best in Boston – to rent or buy – and vary from the predictable (zombie, pirate, superhero) to the surreal (extremely realistic animals, the pope). The store also deals in theatrical makeup, realistic fake facial hair, feathered headdresses, wigs of all colors and styles, and costume undergarments, like hoop skirts, crinolines, and corsets.

"By-the-pound" is a sales event that happens every morning, when bales of unsorted used clothing get unloaded onto the first floor of the building, resulting in a free-for-all dig-through. The cost is usually $2 per pound for whatever you can get your hands on, but on Fridays, it's only $1 per pound. On weekend days, they open two bales instead of the usual single bale.

Eventually, the clothing buyers for the vintage and costume shops on the other floors sort through, tidy up, and price what is left after the scavenger hunt, distributing it throughout the rest of the store. So this is your one daily chance to get a real bargain.

But if you prefer a less frenzied, more curated experience, there are bargains to be found in the rest of the store, where departments are arranged elegantly by decade, gender, and types of clothing. It's very hard to visit The Garment District without finding something you'll want to take home with you. But even if you leave empty handed, you'll probably have experimented with 10 different possible new looks that you could be sporting – if you only dared.

Address 200 Broadway, Cambridge, MA 02139, +1 (617) 876-5230, www.garmentdistrict.com, service@garmentdistrict.com | **Getting there** Subway to Kendall/MIT (Red Line) | **Hours** Sun–Fri 11am–8pm, Sat 9am–8pm | **Tip** Ever wondered what Dante Alighieri, renowned expert on Hell, looked like? The Dante Alighieri Society has a statue of him right in front and offers regular events celebrating his legacy (41 Hampshire Street, Cambridge, www.dantemass.org).

51 Giant Baby Heads
No cheek-pinching allowed

You don't even have to step inside of the Museum of Fine Arts to behold two of its most curious, arresting, and cute-as-a-button pieces. Named *Day and Night,* these massive bronze baby heads stand eight feet tall, greeting visitors at the MFA's Fenway entrance with a mix of innocence and intrigue.

Spanish artist Antonio López García drew inspiration from his four grandchildren for the sculptures, two of which are located at Madrid's Atocha train station and were installed after the 2004 train bombings in the city as a captivating tribute. The Boston babies, each of which weighs quite a bit more than the average infant (1.65 tons to be exact) were transported from Spain in 2008.

López García is primarily a realist painter, who came to prominence in the 1960s and 1970s through his riveting depictions of ordinary people, objects, interiors, and buildings, as well as panoramic views of Madrid. In addition to works on display at the MFA, his paintings can be found at the Museum of Modern Art in New York and the Museo Nacional Centro de Arte Reina Sofía in Madrid.

A detail that might not be apparent to the casual viewer is that, as their namesakes reflect, one baby is asleep and the other is awake. The level of facial detail for such a large sculpture is incredible, if not a bit disconcerting, but it also makes for perhaps the weirdest and best photo op in all of Boston.

In case you were wondering, the MFA takes good care of their kids. Once a year, the tot heads get a bath in the form of a non-ionic soap that preserves their wax coating. The museum's staff have also been known to dress up the sculptures for the weather or to reflect current events – for example, accessorizing them with woolen hats in the wintertime. More recently, a guerilla artist created larger-than-life masks for the babies during the Coronavirus pandemic.

Address 465 Huntington Avenue, Boston, MA 02115, +1 (617) 267-9300, www.mfa.org |
Getting there Subway to Ruggles (Orange Line) or Museum of Fine Arts (Green "E" Line) |
Hours Unrestricted for sculptures; see website for museum hours | Tip Take your actual
little ones to a play, a musical, or an acting class at Wheelock Family Theatre (180 Riverway,
Boston, www.wheelockfamilytheatre.org).

52 Giant Hockey Stick
What the puck??

As you're driving on the Massachusetts Turnpike toward downtown, between Newton and Cambridge, cast your eyes quickly to the right, and you'll see an enormous, brightly lit building that looks a little bit like a cruise ship, with a large, red "NB" (for "New Balance") on one end. If the light is just right, you'll also note a strangely-angled stick on the right-hand side of the building. It's almost the same height as the building, but it's not holding anything up. In fact, it looks like it's tipping over. It makes no sense. But don't try to figure it out from the highway. Go look at it up close.

When you do so, you'll discover that it's actually a 68-foot sculpture of a hockey stick connecting with a puck of similar scale at ground level. This 7,000-pound, steel stick was fabricated by local ironworkers to stand at attention outside the Warrior Ice Arena, home base and practice space for the Bruins, Boston's beloved hockey team. And possibly for you too! That's right – this brand new, top-of-the-line facility built for one of the best hockey teams in the NHL is open to the general public to use for everything from youth team practices to weddings. There are league events, open skate hours, camps, clinics, and lessons for skaters of all ages interested in building skill on the ice. Professional skaters can sign up for off-season training sessions, and there's even a (somewhat pricey) option to reserve the whole rink for a private skate.

The arena is part of a sports-focused complex that includes New Balance's corporate headquarters and an outlet store, as well as the Bruins' corporate offices and rink.

The ice skating is as good as it gets here, and it's worth keeping your eye on the giant hockey stick. Though only the third largest hockey stick on Earth, it gets a new paint job every August to match the line of sticks the Bruins play with that year.

Address 90 Guest Street, Brighton, MA 02135, +1 (617) 927-7467, www.warrioricearena.com, events@warrioricearena.com | Getting there Bus 64 to Life Street & Guest Street, bus 86 to Market & Vineland Street; Framingham Commuter Rail to Brighton Landing | Hours See website for classes and open public skate sessions | Tip Would you rather skate to a beat? Go to Boston's absolute favorite roller rink, Chez Vous (11 Rhoades Street, Mattapan, www.chezvousrollerrink.com).

53 Graffiti Alley

Spray it, don't say it

Central Square has its fair share of colorful characters, but this small pedestrian pathway gives them a run for their money. A vibrant, stained glass canopy adds beautiful light and shadow to an already fascinating palette of ever-changing spray-painted pieces. You have to look up, down, and all around to truly appreciate the creativity at work. No centimeter is spared, and you're sure to notice something new with every single visit. On the other side is a permanent photo collage of Central's most notable people and places, creating a true tribute to the neighborhood.

Artist Geoff Hargadon and restaurateur Gary Strack established the project in 2007, reaching out to artists around the world to christen the then-bare wall that connects Massachusetts Avenue to a parking lot. Strack's now-shuttered restaurant, Central Kitchen, abutted the 80-foot-long alley (formally known as Modica Way), so it was the perfect opportunity to add a pop of personality and give street artists a dedicated space to showcase their masterpieces without fear of being arrested. Over the years, the wall has attracted both renowned artists like Shepard Fairey, Judith Supine, and Gaia, along with inspired locals hoping to make their mark. It's even the subject of a recent documentary by local filmmaker Olivia Huang.

If you're lucky, you might just encounter a talented artist, aerosol can in hand, in the midst of creating a new mural during your visit. But if you're hoping to capture a particularly Instagram-worthy piece, make sure to act fast; it might just be replaced with a brand new one by next week. There's an unspoken rule among the artists, however, that if you can't improve upon a piece that's there, it's best to leave it alone out of respect. The wall has also become a go-to spot for lightning-fast tributes to celebrities after their passing, including Anthony Bourdain and Kobe Bryant.

Address 565 Massachusetts Avenue, Cambridge, MA 02139 | Getting there Subway to Central (Red Line) | Hours Unrestricted | Tip Sift through the stacks at the longstanding Cheapo Records across the street (538 Massachusetts Avenue, Cambridge, MA 02139, www.cheaporecords.com).

54 Great Brink's Robbery Site

They worked hard for the money

In 1950, more than $1.2 million in cash and $1.5 million in checks were stolen from the Brink's Armored Car depot in the North End, making it the largest robbery in US history at the time. Far from a spontaneous cash grab, the heist was carefully planned and orchestrated by more than 11 individuals. You can imagine the goings on for yourself at what is now a parking garage that gives no hints of the nefarious activities that took place within its walls seven decades earlier.

Behind it all was Anthony Pino, better known as "Fats." This career criminal enlisted the men to case the joint for 18 months to determine the best moment to strike. Making the final, successful attempt even spookier, the robbers donned Navy peacoats and chauffeur's caps that matched the Brink's uniform, along with Halloween masks. They quieted their footsteps with crepe- or rubber-soled boots.

On the night of January 17, it was go time. The posse broke in through at least three locked doors, and five unlucky Brink's employees were held at gunpoint and pushed to the floor, mouths taped and hands tied behind their backs. The men stacked the cash in bags outside the building's entrance and made their escape.

Amazingly, all living guilty parties were eventually identified and charged. It took six years, however, because initial clues were limited to one of the chauffeurs' caps, a rope, and the victims' testimonies. In the end, it was selfishness and greed that did them all in. One of the men, Joseph James O'Keefe, came clean and broke the case open after multiple attempts were made on his life due to squabbles with his co-conspirators over fair shares of the loot. A mere five days before the statute of limitations expired, six men were arrested, with two more nabbed four months later – the other two had already passed away.

Address 632-698 Commercial Street, Boston, MA 02109 | Getting there Subway to Aquarium (Blue Line) or Haymarket (Green or Orange Line) | Hours Unrestricted | Tip A short walk and a world away from the robbery site is All Saints Way (4 Battery Street, Boston), a small but mighty shrine to the holy figures that's tucked into an alley and covered with prayer cards, figurines, and photos.

55 The Great Molasses Flood
A reminder of a tragic and sticky situation

Before you go to visit this place, do yourself a favor and buy some molasses. It has a distinctive smell that it's worth reminding yourself of as you stand in front of a sign memorializing the day when a tidal wave of molasses came rushing through the streets of Boston, crushing everything in its path.

Without the olfactory aid, it's hard to wrap your brain around the idea of a molasses flood – a veritable tsunami of 2,300,000 gallons of black, sweet goo rushing through the streets at an estimated 35 miles per hour, peaking at heights reported varyingly as 25 and 40 feet.

Here's how it happened: Purity Distilling Company, a company that made ethanol alcohol out of molasses, retained storage facilities at 529 Commercial Street in the North End. They stored molasses arriving here by ship in tanks temporarily and then moved it via pipeline to a processing plant in Cambridge. But sometimes the molasses had to be stored for a longer term than planned. On January 15, 1919, a tank contained molasses that had been there for almost six months and was full nearly to capacity, which was unusual. And so the molasses began to ferment, filling the tank's remaining space with gas. Though January is usually quite cold in Boston, on this date it was about 40 °F (4.5 °C). Also, the 5-story-high metal tank had slight imperfections. It had been leaking here and there but had not received any significant maintenance.

On the day the tank exploded, events happened fast. The molasses burst out of the tank with such force that it ripped the local fire station from its foundation and buckled railroad tracks. 21 people died, and another 150 were seriously injured. It took four days to pull all of the victims from the muck. The damage to the city was in the millions of dollars. Who'd have thought that a substance so sweet could cause such chaos and destruction?

Address 529 Commercial Street, Boston, MA 02109 | **Getting there** Subway to North Station (Orange or Green Line) | **Hours** Daily dawn–dusk | **Tip** The site where the molasses tank once was is now part of the Boston Harborwalk, a 42-mile linear park, and one of the most pleasurable ways to stroll along the city's shoreline. So why not just keep walking? (www.bostonharbornow.org/what-we-do/explore/harborwalk).

56_Harbor Island Secrets

Live out a ferry tale

Choose your own adventure, from swimming and camping to fort exploration, on this urban island chain. While only 7 of the 34 are publicly accessible by ferry, you can easily spend a day on each and stay entertained. As the largest recreational space in Eastern Massachusetts, there are plenty of places to kick back. But it's not all picnics and panoramic views; the islands hide many unexpected stories.

There's Georges Island with Fort Warren, a spooky, stone and granite military base from the Civil War era, and its tales of the Lady in Black. The unsettled spirit is that of a Confederate soldier's wife, Melanie Lanier, who was hanged after she snuck onto the island dressed as a man in an attempt to free her jailed husband. She supposedly haunts visitors, cloaked in the black robe she was wearing when she died. Spectacle Island is a bit less eerie, but it wasn't always that way. It was once the home of a glue factory, hospital, horse-rendering facility, and hotel. And for six decades, it was a garbage dump, which grew into an 80-foot-high trash heap with random methane explosions that illuminated the night sky, like creepy fireworks.

Peddocks Island combines natural beauty and historic intrigue. You'll find Fort Andrews, a former Coast Artillery Post, and a World War II-era chapel. It's all about simple pleasures on Grape Island, which is actually full of wild berries. Bumpkin Island has lived a few different, interesting lives, one as a smelting factory, another as a fish-drying operation. A children's hospital operated there in the early 20th century, the remains of which you can still explore. Thompson's Island, accessible in the summertime, served as a Native American trading post and later, a vocational school for orphan children.

Perhaps the most mysterious island is Lovells. Several ships met their demise here, and it was once in the running to be the location of the Statue of Liberty. Fort Standish adds to its bygone charm.

Address Various, Boston Harbor, www.bostonharborislands.org | Getting there Subway to Aquarium (Blue Line), catch ferries from Long Wharf | Hours See website for ferry schedules | Tip Cruise even further into history with a two-hour narrated lighthouse tour (www.bostonharborislands.org/lighthouse-tours). You'll see Long Island Light, Graves Light, and the country's first light station, Boston Light.

57 Harvard Lampoon Building

They've got jokes

The headquarters of one of the world's longest-running humor magazines is delightfully at odds with the rest of Harvard's more traditional buildings. While its exterior features the classic red brick that's characteristic of the Ivy League institution, quirky design details give you an inkling that there's something a bit different going on here. Namely, the unmistakable purple, yellow, and red door and a façade that resembles someone wearing a Prussian helmet. The *pièce de résistance* is a copper ibis statue that sits atop the roof and has been repeatedly stolen as a running (or rather, flying) gag.

Racking up a whopping $40,000 in construction costs in 1909, the building holds the title of most expensive college newspaper headquarters in the entire country. It's beloved by many, but it hasn't been without its haters. Former Cambridge mayor Alfred Vellucci called it "one of the ugliest buildings in the world," inexplicably compared it to a witch on a broomstick, and at one point tried to declare it as a public urinal. His disdain ran so deep that he even planted a tree in front of the building in 1961 to block the public's view of it.

The man responsible for this supposed abomination? Edmund M. Wheelwright, Boston's former city architect and designer of the Larz Anderson Auto Museum (see ch. 69). His inspirations, which included a Virginia church, were diverse. He even had 7,000 Delft tiles imported from the Netherlands to decorate the Great Hall. It remains the largest display of its kind outside of that country.

All kidding aside, the Lampoon's alumni are a seriously prestigious lot. Among its graduates are writers for *Seinfeld*, *The Simpsons*, *30 Rock*, and *The Office*, comedians Conan O'Brien, B. J. Novak, and Colin Jost, and writers John Updike and George Plimpton.

Address 44 Bow Street, Cambridge, MA 02138, +1 (617) 495-7801, www.harvardlampoon.com, info@harvardlampoon.com | **Getting there** Subway to Harvard (Red Line) | **Hours** Unrestricted from the outside only | **Tip** Keep the giggles going with a knee-slapping and/or gut-busting comedy show at Improv Asylum (216 Hanover Street, Boston, www.improvasylum.com).

58___Harvard Square Theater
Gone but not forgotten – because it's still there

Though a marquee and a mural of theater doors still exists at its address, the actual doors to this former Lowe's Harvard Square Theater have been shuttered since the summer of 2012.

Rumors circulate regularly about it re-opening, and it could happen. This place has had several makeovers since its first identity as the University Theater when it opened in 1926. Back then, the entrance was on Massachusetts Avenue, and the theater seats for 1600+ patrons were made of wicker. The velvet curtains that parted when movies began screening on its original screen had a gigantic painting on them of George Washington taking command of the Continental Army on the Cambridge Common, where it really happened about a block away.

It was a movie theater from the beginning – Alfred Hitchcock and Woody Allen both held special screenings here. But that never stopped it from hosting some very memorable rock concerts. It is rumored that Bruce Springsteen got noticed for the first time by a music critic here after opening for Bonnie Raitt in 1974 as a bit more than a run-of-the-mill performer. Other famous rockers who are known to have graced its stage include Joan Baez, David Bowie, the Clash, Bob Dylan, Hall and Oates, and Iggy Pop. The theater also hosted innumerable magic acts and vaudeville shows.

But the real reason to celebrate the Harvard Square Theater is that this is where the very first live performance of *The Rocky Horror Picture Show* occurred in the US. In fact, it occurred once and then continued to occur here weekly at midnight on Saturday nights for 28 years straight. (Well maybe "straight" is not quite the right word...)

If you're in the area, go pay homage to this place. You may be the first to find that it actually has re-opened for a new iteration. In that case, please let us here at *111 Places That You Must Not Miss* know immediately so that we can all "do the Time Warp again."

Address 10 Church Street, Cambridge, MA 02138 | Getting there Subway to Harvard (Red Line) | Hours Unrestricted | Tip Around the corner is a small and ancient graveyard, the Old Burying Ground (Massachusetts Avenue and Garden Street, Cambridge). Here lies the painter and poet Washington Allston. Notable for, among other things, being the only artist yet whose name has been reassigned to a town in America: Allston, MA just across the river from Cambridge.

59 Hibernian Hall

A storied building

Hibernian Hall in Roxbury has had so many different lives, you'd think it was a cat. Its name comes from its original function as the local headquarters of the Ancient Order of Hibernians. The fraternal organization has its roots in Northern Ireland in the 1800s, but it had mostly transformed into the political activist groups Sinn Féin and the IRA by the early 1900s.

The group is now much more active in the US than Ireland, having hopped over here in 1836 and building Hibernian Hall in 1913. The main criteria for membership are that you have to be male, born or descended from someone born in Ireland, and you have to be Catholic. As the Ancient Order of Hibernians became less active in Boston, the space morphed into more of an Irish-American community center, and then a dance hall with gleaming wood floors and large windows. The ground level is retail, the second floor boasts a large banquet hall, and the third and fourth floors are one concert hall with balconies – perfect for big bands and dance parties. In the 1960s, the building was foreclosed on and then converted to the Opportunities Industrialization Center for international vocational training. But then the building fell into disrepair and was essentially abandoned by the late 1980s. It sat empty and vandalized for over a decade and was then purchased and rehabbed by the Madison Park Development Corporation.

In 2005, it reopened as an arts and cultural hub. It's now an established performing arts destination that has helped revitalize Roxbury. The range of what you'll find here any given week includes everything from Boston's famous "Celebrity Series" of touring performances, to poetry slams, to local dance and theater productions. The emphasis is on multicultural arts programming, but conferences and celebrations occur in the beautifully restored ballroom and theater as well.

Address 184 Dudley Street, Roxbury, MA 02119, +1 (617) 541-3900, www.madison-park.org/
what-we-do/arts-culture/hibernian-hall, hibernianhall@madison-park.org | Getting there
Subway to Roxbury Crossing (Orange Line), Silver Line bus and routes 1, 8, 15, 23, 28, 41, 42,
44, 45, 47, and 66 to Nubian Square | Hours See website for events schedule | Tip Check out
the 500-foot Black Lives Matter street mural painted on Washington Street by local artists
right outside of Black Market (2136 Washington Street, Boston) and if they're open
(www.facebook.com/blackmarketnubian) Black Market itself is not to be missed!

60 The Hood Milk Bottle
You're going to need a bigger glass

What's 40 feet tall and makes you crave chocolate chip cookies? The answer won't come easily to mind unless you happen to be standing outside of Boston's world famous Children's Museum. In that case, you'll know in a heartbeat that it's the Hood Milk Bottle.

In the 1930s, Arthur Gagner, who had an ice-cream shop in Taunton, MA, came up with the kooky (not cookie!) idea of building a gigantic milk bottle as an advertising scheme. And so he made his idea come to life, building the enormous bottle out of wood. And people came to see his milk bottle and buy his ice cream, as he hoped they would. His was actually one of the first fast food drive-in restaurants in the United States. But when Ganger retired, he stopped being able to repair and otherwise maintain the outsized milk bottle. It became an eyesore. The dairy company H. P. Hood & Sons, Inc. bought the bottle, and they decided to donate it to the Boston Children's Museum. The bottle was shipped from Taunton to Boston and installed in its current location in 1977.

Over the years, the milk bottle has served up a variety of different Boston favorites, including the beloved lobster rolls from Sullivan's of Castle Island. It has also had movies projected on its side. But most likely its true function is to fuel children for high octane play. The concession booth, which serves up high-carb ice cream and hot dogs, has a phrase across the outside that reads, "It's Hoods be Good."

It's definitely not very easy to be good when it comes to delicious ice cream. You really just need to bounce off of some walls when that sugar high kicks in, which is okay because the milk bottle happens to be conveniently placed strategically in front of the entrance to the Children's Museum. Just open the front door to the museum and let your children bounce right into the three-story-high New Balance Foundation climbing structure.

Address Hood Milk Bottle Plaza, South Boston, MA 02210, +1 (617) 426-6500, www.bostonchildrensmuseum.org, info@bostonchildrensmuseum.org | **Getting there** Subway to South Station (Red Line) | **Hours** See website for hours | **Tip** Your best bet for cookies in the area is going to be Flour Bakery (2 Farnsworth Street, Boston, www.flourbakery.com), a small local chain known for its delectable, French-inspired baked goods.

61 Houdini Plaque

Where Harry Houdini escaped Boston's dirty water

On May 1, 1908, likely still quite cold in Boston, 20,000+ people gathered on the Harvard Bridge, which spans Massachusetts Avenue from the Massachusetts Institute of Technology (MIT) in Cambridge to the Back Bay area of Boston. They were there to watch the world's most famous escape artist plunge to his potential, watery death.

Houdini's hands were cuffed behind his back and bound to a chain around his neck. On a signal from a boat nearby, he dropped 30 feet into Boston's most notoriously dirty water, the Charles River (although the water probably wasn't dirty enough to be harmful to his health). Forty seconds ticked by as the crowd held its collective breath. And then Houdini emerged, chainless and unscathed!

Houdini not only lived to tell the tale, but once warm and dry, he performed a full two-week run of shows at B. F. Keith's theater, a major and glamorous venue on the Keith Vaudeville Circuit that is now the Boston Opera House. The leap was a publicity stunt for the shows, and it was Boston's still quite active branch of the Society of American Magicians that was kind enough to make sure the spot was marked for posterity. Pictures of the plunge, in the form of magic lantern slides, can be found online on the Library of Congress' website.

The plaque is very close to the top of the Massachusetts Avenue ramp that offers a connection for walkers, bikers and wheelchairs between the bridge and the Charles River's rambling paths below, so it's very easy to find if you're looking for it. It makes for a quick side-bar to any day spent hanging out along the river, which is a very good way to spend any nice day in Boston. If you're bringing kids by to take a look, make sure to give them the whole "don't try this at home" talk. And if you find the plaque inspiring, then you will surely enjoy a lecture or other event about magic hosted by the Boston Society of American Magicians.

HARRY HOUDINI
(Ehrich Weiss)
1874–1926

In memoriam to the great Artist
and Past National President who performed
one of his well known escapes from this bridge
on May 1, 1908.

Society of American Magicians
Boston Assembly Number 9

Metropolitan District Commission
Harvard Bridge, Boston, May 1, 1994

Address Boston side of Harvard Bridge, Massachusetts Avenue, Boston, MA 02115, www.facebook.com/SAM9Boston | Getting there Bus 1 to Beacon Street | Hours Unrestricted | Tip If you stay on that same side of the bridge and walk towards Cambridge, you'll notice markings at regular intervals measuring out "smoots," measurement of the bridge in units equivalent to the height of one Oliver Smoot, an MIT grad in the early 1960s. He became chairman of the American National Standards Institute, which regulates units of measurement.

62 Indoor Lightning Storms
It's electrifying at the MOS

It turns out that lightning does strike twice – and again, and again – at the Museum of Science's (MOS) Theater of Electricity. This equally educational and entertaining space is home to the world's largest air-insulated Van de Graaff generator, an electrostatic device originally created to aid in physics research by accelerating subatomic particles. There are smaller versions at museums around the world, like the American Museum of Science and Energy in Oak Ridge, Tennessee and the SPARK Museum of Electrical Invention in Bellingham, Washington. But you'll find the most giant edition at MOS. Its vibrant colors and grand stature give it a fantastical, *Wizard of Oz*-like quality. No matter whether you're young or old, a bona fide science geek, or someone who just appreciates stuff that looks really cool, you're in for a treat when you attend a demonstration.

Its namesake is Dr. Robert Van de Graaff, a physicist who invented the generator in 1929. The model at the MOS, which dates back to 1931, features two massive columns topped with spheres that tower at 40 feet tall. In its previous life, it was actively used for radiography and nuclear medicine research at MIT before moving to its permanent home here in the 1950s.

Up to five million volts of electricity can be exchanged between the globes through a moving belt inside the machine, which results in crackling lightning bolts. It's basically a much more dramatic version of what happens when you rub your socks on the rug to create some static shock. Museum educators specially trained in operating the larger-than-life apparatus lead presentations for all ages about electromagnetic force, thunderstorms, safety, and more.

While the generator is the *pièce de résistance*, the theater also houses Tesla coils that produce incredible high-frequency visuals with up to half a million volts.

Address 1 Museum of Science Driveway, Boston, MA 02114, +1 (617) 723-2500, www.mos.org |
Getting there Subway to Lechmere (Green "E" Line) | Hours Sun–Thu 9am–5pm,
Fri 9am–9pm, Sat 9am–5pm | Tip Get out of the storm and into nature with a visit to
nearby Lechmere Canal Park (Cambridge, www.tclf.org/landscapes/lechmere-canal-park),
where shade-giving trees and a pretty fountain provide a tranquil escape.

63 The Italian Donkey

A strange souvenir

It happens to the best of us: we go on vacation, find ourselves utterly charmed by something in a gift shop, and then – boom – everyone we know gets a tacky, shell-shaped soap dish advertising a seaside village they've never been to. But if anyone complains about their thoughtful gift, tell them the story of this donkey. They'll be instantly grateful that your budget was small and luggage space limited.

Once upon a time, in the 1990s, a man named Roger Webb was on a trip to Florence. Webb had some extra *lire* in his pocket that he was looking to spend on something that would remind him of his time there. He found and fell in love with a small bronze statue of a donkey...which he bought for the equivalent of $10,000. If you saw this donkey, you might agree that it is $10,000 worth of cuteness. In fact, you *can* see it because Webb didn't buy it for his daughter or his nephew. He bought it for the City of Boston.

When Webb returned home and offered this sweet bronze burro to Boston, the city was as nonplussed as whomever you'd tell this story to would be about their new cross-stitched Martha's Vineyard toilet seat cover. But Webb was determined to change the city's mind. He finally figured out that it wasn't that the city didn't *like* the donkey, it just didn't have any context for it. Webb could fix that!

With a little help from a cousin, a sculptor who had some skill at casting bronze, Webb turned the donkey into a work of conceptual art, explaining that it represented Boston's long, long history of electing its leaders from the Democratic Party. He added a pair of bronze footprints facing the donkey so that Republicans could come and yell at it. City officials eventually gave in and said yes.

So vacation impulse buying is why Boston has a small Italian donkey and a pair of bronze footprints standing in front of our Old City Hall. It is *really* cute though.

Address 45 School Street, Boston, MA 02108 | **Getting there** Subway to Park Street (Red or Green Line) | **Hours** Unrestricted | **Tip** Why not visit the donkey on your way to or from a long night of dancing at one of Boston's favorite gay bars, The Alley (14 Pl Alley, Boston, www.thealleybar.com)?

64 Jackson's Sawed-Off Head

A presidential pardon?

Okay, it's not his *actual* head, but it's the sentiment that counts. Back in 1833, President Andrew Jackson was less than popular in the Whig-lovin' city of Boston, so you can imagine the displeasure among citizens when the USS *Constitution,* aka "Old Ironsides," was adorned with a wooden figurehead of Jackson. It replaced one of Hercules to commemorate his new honorary doctorate of laws degree from Harvard.

Rather than sit idle and grumble about the abomination, Captain Samuel Dewey took matters into his own hands on a stormy July night the following year. Armed with a saw, he allegedly took a boat out to the ship and sliced halfway through the seventh president's wood noggin, leaving a somewhat gruesome looking mouth and chin attached to the body due to the placement of an impenetrable metal rod. The perpetrator remained at large for just a few days, at which time Dewey stepped up and claimed responsibility.

While it's unclear if it was due to his unbearable guilt or some other motivation, Captain Dewey actually attempted to return the stolen head to Jackson himself after coming clean. Can you imagine receiving a more twisted gift than a dismantled replica of your own head? Anyway, there was one small problem: the president was too sick to receive any visitors. Instead, Vice President Martin Van Buren met with Dewey and demanded to hear all the sordid details of the partial decapitation. He tried desperately to have Dewey arrested for his misdeed, but, unsurprisingly, there was no law against such a strangely specific act.

As a memento (and because you have to keep a sense of humor about these sorts of things) one of Dewey's pals created a plaster cast of the bust, which sits on display today at the USS Constitution Museum along with a small fragment of the original artifact. The rest of it can be found at the Museum of the City of New York.

Address USS Constitution Museum, Building 22, Charlestown Navy Yard, Charlestown, MA 02129, +1 (617) 426-1812, www.ussconstitutionmuseum.org | Getting there Subway to Community College (Orange Line) | Hours See website for seasonal hours | Tip While you're at the museum, it only makes sense to see the place where everything went down. Climb aboard the USS *Constitution* itself (3rd Street, Boston), the oldest commissioned ship in the US Navy.

Mystery Solved!

This wooden fragment was cherished by the family who acquired it thirty years ago. They wondered if the story they were told was true. Was it really a piece of CONSTITUTION's Andrew Jackson figurehead vandalized 150 years earlier?

The mystery was solved on national television when the History Detectives came to the scene of the crime and reunited these lips with the rest of the head to prove its authenticity.

Museum Purchase, Commodores Fund [2180.1]

The Legend of the Headless Figurehead

Andrew Jackson became President in 1829, but was unpopular in New England. Despite this, a figurehead of

65 Jamaica Pond Taco Bench

Sometimes it's just easier to stand

Jamaica Pond is a lovely place to spend an afternoon. In nice weather, you can take boats out on the water, jog, bike, or stroll around the path that encircles the pond. Or simply sit on a bench and people-watch. But not every bench.

Though most of the benches at Jamaica Pond operate the traditional way (horizontal part to sit on, vertical part to lean back on), one of the benches at Jamaica Pond is a bit off. Actually, a lot off. It looks exactly like all of the other benches, except that it's U-shaped instead of L-shaped. It's basically shaped like a taco.

Do people sit on it? Yes. At least they try. A quick search on Instagram for #tacobench will prove quickly that people that cannot resist folding themselves up and taking selfies with their arms and legs sticking out of the bench, pretending to be the taco's filling. But that's not why the bench is there.

The bench is there because Boston is home to a small handful of conceptual artists, one of whom, Matthew Hincman, lived close by the pond in 2006. Hincman, it seems, was unable to resist making fun of the pond's other less-creative benches, calling them all out on their conformity by surreptitiously planting this one in their midst. God only knows where he got the bench parts and chutzpah to do it, but the City of Boston, showing off its usually quite well-concealed sense of humor, left the bench in place. Well, that's not true. First they removed it, but then they put it back. Hincman just had to go through all of the proper channels for creating public art before it was allowed to stay.

The moral of the story is that Boston needed a taco bench but didn't know it until it had one. And you too need a taco bench in your life. You just don't know it yet. So go visit this one and cram yourself into it in some way. Just think of it as a free chiropractor.

Address Jamaica Pond, Jamaica Plain, MA 02130, www.emeraldnecklace.org/park-overview/jamaica-pond | Getting there Subway to Green Street (Orange Line), enter the path at Pond Street, near the boathouse and turn right | Hours Daily dawn–dusk | Tip Inspired to make an unusual bench of your own? Take an accessible-to-all-ages class in woodworking (or better yet "tinkering and inventing") nearby at The Eliot School (24 Eliot Street, Jamaica Plain, www.eliotschool.org).

66 JFK's Birthplace

Pop by where JFK popped out

All great leaders have to start somewhere, and like most of us, they usually start in wombs. Though President John F. Kennedy has a whole (and really great) library and museum in Dorchester that you should not miss, you can also go visit the humbler place where JFK left the particular womb that hosted his earliest development. Some presidents are born in hospitals, and some, like JFK, are born at home. In those cases, their homes, even if just set alongside a bunch of other homes on a tree-lined street, may become museums.

It's a cozy house and a cozy museum. You can see the actual master bedroom where the 35th President of the United States was born, the actual piano where he practiced his piano lessons as a child, and the actual pot that his Boston baked beans were cooked in – all while listening to an audio tour narrated by his mother, Rose Fitzgerald Kennedy. And Rose Kennedy is more than just your tour guide and JFK's mother. She's the visionary and creator of this tender museum.

In 1966, after her son's untimely death, the Kennedy family bought the house back from its owners at the time so that Mrs. Kennedy could recreate the small, nine-room house's 1917 interior. She hired a department store decorator to help her stage the home as she remembered it, using personal furnishings and family belongings in all of the house's main rooms. It's essentially a living memorial to her son and the days when the whole Kennedy family was intact, innocent, and looking forward to a bright future.

If you want a sense of Kennedy as a president, go to the John F. Kennedy Library and Museum. But if you want a sense of him as a son and the rare experience of seeing an important historical figure through a mother's eyes, visit this one. Small and free to the public, it's a history museum and also a museum of motherhood. Maybe this is what all museums would be like if it were always Mother's Day.

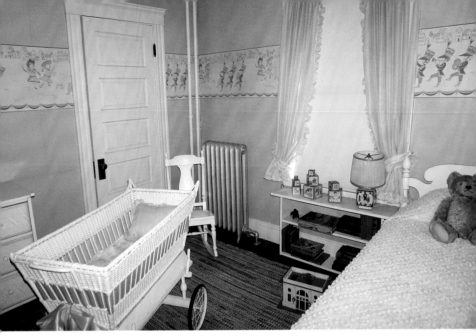

Address 83 Beals Street, Brookline, MA 02446, +1 (617) 566-7937, www.nps.gov/nr/travel/presidents/john_f_kennedy_birthplace.html | Getting there Subway to Coolidge Corner (Green "C" Line) | Hours See website | Tip Fun fact: JFK was the inspiration for many songs, including ones by the Byrds, Lou Reed, The Beach Boys, and even Pearl Jam. Chances are high you can find them all at Village Vinyl & HiFi (307 Harvard Street, Brookline, www.villagevinylhifi.com).

67 King Philip's War

You'd never know it happened here

Boston is the birthplace of the US. It's where tea was thrown over-board, where the American Revolution began, where independence was declared. But before colonists could turn their energy towards freeing themselves from the tyranny of Great Britain, they had to do a bit of oppressing themselves.

There were many Native groups in New England, but the two that first had contact with Europeans in the Boston area were the Massachusett (meaning "big mountain," in reference to the Great Blue Hills), and the Wampanoag ("Easterners" or "people of the dawn"). The earliest (Dutch) map to note these tribes in this area – called "New Amsterdam" at the time – was created in 1614, which is about when European contact started to impact Native populations, introducing novel diseases with mortality rates as high as 90%. Natives taught immigrants from the UK about farming and fishing techniques appropriate to the region, but it was actually the rapid decline in their numbers that allowed the colonies to really thrive here.

Despite massive losses, the original Bostonians did not give in quickly or easily. In 1675, Wampanoag Chief Metacom ("King Philip") led an armed rebellion against American colonists that raged for two years. It's still considered the deadliest war in US history in proportion to population and left 60–80% of New England's remaining Native population dead or sold into slavery. The colonists killed King Philip and mounted his head on a pike in public for 25 years. They chopped up his body and hung it in the trees.

There are ongoing calls to place a memorial on Boston Common. For now, you can come and do your reflecting on Boston's violent past at The Great Elm, where many Native Americans, including a famous Nipmuc healer Tantamous, were executed. Look for the plaque at the foot of the tree, facing the the Frog Pond.

Address Enter Boston Common at the intersection of Tremont and West Streets. The exact site is marked on virtual maps as "The Great Elm." | **Getting there** Subway to Park Street (Red or Green Line) | **Hours** Daily dawn–dusk | **Tip** Interested in supporting or tracking the progress of the effort to memorialize Metacom? Connect with the North American Indian Center of Boston in Jamaica Plain. They've been doing advocacy work and hosting cultural events since the late 1960s (105 South Huntington Avenue, Jamaica Plain, www.naicob.org).

68 Langone Park Bocce Courts

Eight can play this game

Between its homey cappuccino cafés and classic red-sauce Italian eateries, spending a day in the North End always feels an awful lot like stepping back into the past. And there are few better ways to keep that Old World feeling alive than with a rousing game of bocce. In fact, considering that the ball sport traces all the way back to the Roman Empire before catching on with Italian immigrants and just about everyone else who appreciates a good game of lawn bowling, it's probably as ancient as you can go these days without a time machine.

Langone Park, which was established in 1973, is also home to a Little League baseball field and a playground for children, but the three courts (or *campos*, if you want to be proper about it) are the main attraction. Beyond just providing the space to play, they also offer amazing views of the adjacent harbor, US Navy vessel *Old Ironsides*, and the Bunker Hill Monument that might just throw you off your game if you aren't careful. All are welcome to play for free so long as they bring their own set of balls. That's the beauty of the whole thing: families, couples, and college kids mingling with feisty North End elders and whoever else decides to drop by that afternoon.

Once you're ready to take your commitment to the sport up a notch from a casual Sunday game amongst friends, check out the neighborhood's Major League organization, where every match is followed by a well-earned beer or three at a local watering hole. Feeling more spectator than sporty? The court-side seating is ideal for sipping your macchiato, munching on a cannoli, and cheering on your best bocce buddy. On second thought, perhaps a molasses cookie would be more appropriate; the park encompasses much of the area where the famously sticky-sweet flood occurred in 1919 (see ch. 55).

Address 529-543 Commercial Street, Boston, MA 02109, +1 (617) 626-1250,
majorleaguebocce.com/boston | Getting there Subway to Haymarket (Orange or Green Line)
or Aquarium (Blue Line) | Hours Daily dawn–dusk | Tip The only thing better than some
authentic bocce is some authentic pizza. Since 1965, the family-owned Galleria Umberto
(289 Hanover Street, Boston) has been serving up cash-only slices 'til they run out. Get there
early to get in on the action.

69 Larz Anderson Auto Museum

Get your motor running

A veritable castle of cars that looks more glam than garage, the Larz Anderson Auto Museum is the oldest collection of automobiles in the nation. The museum began as the personal hobby of Brookline socialites Larz and Isabel Anderson. Larz was a well-to-do diplomat, and Isabel became the wealthiest female in America at just five years old as the heiress to a shipping and railroad fortune. She was also the first woman in Massachusetts to receive a driver's license.

The two lovebirds, who shared a passion for expensive automobiles, went on a lengthy spree from 1899 to 1948 and purchased 32 vehicles, 14 of which are on display today. They'd show off their acquisitions on Sunday afternoons to friends who visited their ritzy estate. Larz died in 1937, and upon Isabel's passing in 1948, she requested that the collection be given over to the Veteran Motor Car Club of America, which would establish a nonprofit and the museum as it's known today. Among the beauties in the current collection are a 1926 Lincoln, a 1907 Fiat, a 1905 Electromobile, and a 1925 Luxor Taxi.

Even if you're not a gearhead, the building's impressive architecture alone is worth a visit. There's good reason it looks so regal: the carriage house was designed in 1888 by Boston's then city architect, Edmund M. Wheelwright, whose work can also be seen at the Longfellow Bridge, Boston Opera House, and Harvard Lampoon Building (see ch. 57). Just across the street is Larz Anderson Park, with well-manicured gardens, walking paths, and an ice skating rink in the winter.

The museum hosts shows on the lawn, including Cars & Coffee events on Saturday mornings that gather owners to talk shop. Transporterfest features plenty of decked-out Volkswagen vans that would suit the Scooby-Doo gang or a pack of Deadheads nicely.

Address 15 Newton Street, Brookline, MA 02445, +1 (617) 522-6547, www.larzanderson.org | Getting there Bus 51 to Clyde Street & Whitney Street | Hours Tue–Sat 10am–4pm, Sun 9am–3pm | Tip After you gaze at luxury cars, graze on the elegant tasting menu at Ten Tables (597 Centre Street, Jamaica Plain, www.tentables.net).

70 Liberty Hotel
A jail gone upscale

Fortunately, the most you'll be in for is a few nights at this jail-house-turned-luxury-hotel. Opened in 1851 and constructed in the Boston Granite style, the Charles Street Jail was a joint effort between renowned architect Gridley James Fox Bryant and Reverend Louis Dwight. The result was a grand, light-filled space with facets of Romanesque and Renaissance architecture that eschewed the bleak prison stereotype. The inmates were also anything but typical: Malcolm X and Sacco and Vanzetti were among the famous names who got locked up here.

Despite its pretty appearance, it wasn't all skylights and rainbows. A combination of overcrowding and substandard living conditions led to a revolt and a declaration of constitutional rights violations in 1973, but it wasn't until the end of 1990 that the jail was fully vacated. The building was purchased by Mass General Hospital the next year, and in 2001, work to transform the property began. In 2007, the Liberty Hotel finally opened its doors to the public.

Many distinctive elements of the prison remain, including the breathtaking central atrium. A cupola, removed during construction in 1949, was rebuilt from scratch to be meticulously accurate to Bryant's original design. The hotel's bars and eateries, bearing playful names like Alibi and Clink, retained the original cells, guests-only retreat Catwalk sits on the same "runway" where inmates once walked, and the outdoor exercise area is now a chic courtyard lounge.

Even new features incorporate nods to the jail, like the exposed brick and "Crime does not pay" poster that hangs in fine dining restaurant Scampo (Italian for "escape"). And each of the 298 guest rooms combine history with luxury, from the deluxe rooms to the suites with Charles River views. Don't plan on staying the night? You can still take a guided tour to dive into the Liberty's former life.

Address 215 Charles Street, Boston, MA 02114, +1 (617) 224-4000, www.libertyhotel.com, reservations@libertyhotel.com | Getting there Subway to Charles/MGH (Red Line) | Hours Unrestricted | Tip Mosey on over to Louisburg Square to explore more of Beacon Hill's dark side, at the site of the Debutante Murder (85 Pinckney Street, Boston), the home where the pregnant niece of actor Montgomery Clift shot and killed her boyfriend in 1962 after he refused to marry her.

71 The Lilypad

Arts and drafts

Indie outfits, jazz musicians, classical performers, and artists who defy categorization take center stage at this intimate Inman Square venue that unites art aficionados from the neighborhood and beyond. On any given night, you might wander in to witness a kinetic performance by a surf rock band, a low-key poetry reading, or a stand-up comedian working on new material.

The single-room space manages to pack in an amazing amount of charm and character, due in large part to artist Dan Masi's colorful, rotating wall murals that incorporate elements of folklore and mythology – they're as engaging as the performances themselves. Between the DIY vibe of the benches and folding chairs and a quaint cash bar, where staff serve up craft beer, hard cider, wine, and soft drinks, stepping into The Lilypad immediately gives you the sense that you've stumbled upon something truly special. It's as if you've suddenly become part of a movie scene taking place in an impossibly cool, snug, and magical local hangout that can't actually exist in real life. But fortunately, it does.

According to Daniel Sarver, The Lilypad's director of operations, this authenticity is a direct byproduct of its core mission. Since its opening in 2005, the venue has been committed to being "A locally owned, artist-run space focused on providing relevant and important musical and artistic performances." Its priority, he adds, is providing "a home for underrepresented artists" as well as "a gathering place for the community of Inman Square" that focuses on "eclectic programming, featuring avant-garde and experimental music." So whether you're seeking a place to debut your new one-woman show, you want to take piano lessons in the most whimsical place, or you're just hoping to discover your new favorite singer-songwriter, you're likely to find what you're looking for right here at The Lilypad.

Address 1353 Cambridge Street, Cambridge, MA 02139, www.lilypadinman.com | Getting there Subway to Central (Red Line); bus 69 or 91 to Cambridge Street & Prospect Street, or bus 83 to Hampshire Street & Cambridge Street | Hours See website for events | Tip If music is one way to escape, then meditating is another. Get your zen on at the Cambridge Insight Meditation Center (331 Broadway, Cambridge, www.cambridgeinsight.org), just a few blocks away.

72 _The Living Room Project_

Art patrons aren't the only kinds of collectors

The Isabella Stewart Gardner Museum is well known for many things: its beautiful courtyard, its famous unsolved art heist, and its strict rules about not making any changes to the collection assembled by its original curator, Isabella Stewart Gardner. But showing art contemporary to the 21st century is not among those things.

In fact, in recent years the museum has been finding subtle, creative ways to curate contemporary art within the constraints of its charter, including hosting process-based work that doesn't stay in the space continuously. One such piece of art is *The Living Room Project* by Taiwanese artist Lee Mingwei. Mingwei isolates what seem like run-of-the-mill, everyday experiences, and he uses them to highlight moments of connection between people.

The Living Room Project evolved out of Mingwei's residency at the museum. It began as a temporary installation in 2000 of an actual living room at the Gardner, where Mingwei invited museum visitors and staff to gather and hang out with him and talk – in particular, about objects included in the décor, echoing Isabella Stewart Gardner's once renowned salons.

But *The Living Room Project* persists long after Mingwei's temporary installation was dismantled. Twice a week, Boston-area residents act as "living room hosts" in the museum's New Wing, sharing, as Isabella Stewart Gardner did, objects from a personal collection that they maintain.

Originally the invitations to share a collection went out only to local artists, but then the circle expanded, and now well over 400 people have shared their personal obsessions with strangers. Entry to these events is free, but the museum does not list them on their website. So you'll have to call to find out when they're scheduled. But it's worth the extra effort to see someone's massive cupcake or glass eye collection, up close.

Address 25 Evans Way, Boston, MA 02115, +1 (617) 566-1401, www.gardnermuseum.org/about/living-room-project, information@isgm.org | Getting there Subway to the Museum of Fine Arts (Green "E" Line) or to Ruggles (Orange Line) | Hours Wed–Mon 11am–5pm | Tip If you're seeking more contemporary art, saunter around the corner and check out Boston's new MassArt Art Museum (MAAM) (621 Huntington Avenue, Boston, www.maam.massart.edu). It's free!

73 Lynch Family Skatepark
Half pipes, full hearts, can't lose

If your extreme sports experience is limited to a few games of *Tony Hawk's Pro Skater* and watching the X Games once, fear not. You can live vicariously through the kickflippers and ollie masters at this 40,000-square-foot park, where the terrain includes steps, ledges, and bowls that resemble empty swimming pools.

A true labor of love, the project was actually the brainchild of *Make Way for Ducklings* artist Nancy Schön (see cover), whose *The Tortoise and The Hare* sculpture was serving a second purpose as a practice spot for area skateboarders. Her initial annoyance soon turned to sympathy as she discovered that the skaters were not purposely trying to damage her art; they just had nowhere else to go. And so began a decade-plus undertaking, with the input of both local and legendary extreme athletes, including Andy Macdonald, who hails from Melrose. Lynch's long-awaited opening in 2015 was equally star studded, with Tony Alva and Ray Barbee at the ceremony.

The park's stark, concrete jungle vibes perfectly complement its location under a Zakim Bridge ramp, the zooming of skateboards and cars joining in perfect harmony to create a true symphony of the city (with a few "dudes," "brahs," and expletives thrown in for good measure). It also doubles as a primo place for photographers seeking unique muses. Not only are there ample opportunities for action shots, but the subjects are more than happy to ham it up and show off their tricks for the cameras. Just make sure to keep your wits about you to avoid flying boards, bikes, and helmets.

Keep an eye out for subtle nods to the sport's history throughout, from the checkered Vans area to a recreation of "the hospital bank," a go-to structure for local skaters back in the day. Of course, Schön gets her very own shoutout, too, with large etchings of *The Tortoise and The Hare* sculpture to remind shredders where it all began.

Address Education Street, Cambridge, MA 02141, +1 (617) 608-1410, www.thecharles.org/
our-work/lynch-family-skatepark | Getting there Subway to Lechmere (Green "E" Line)
or Community College (Orange Line) | Hours Daily dawn–9pm | Tip If you want to be
taken seriously as a skater, the right gear is key. One Gig (367 Washington Street, Boston,
www.onegigco.com), Boston's self-proclaimed "skateboarding shredquarters" has you covered.

74 The Magic Nail

If they don't win, blame the nail

There's being superstitious, and then there's attributing a slew of major league sports wins to a small nail. But this *is* Boston, after all, and the craziest ideas have a funny way of proving successful here – especially when it comes to athletics. The incredible story, which native Bostonian Joe Limone originally shared with *The Moth Radio Hour*, began with a childhood friend's life-threatening freak accident in 2001. After being nearly pierced to death by a nail that fell out of a 2x4 at the construction site of Gillette Stadium, Limone's friend Lou asked the doctors for the pointy weapon as a morbid keepsake and reminder of his immense good fortune.

To pay it forward, Lou and Joe devised a wacky plan: hide the nail somewhere in Foxboro Stadium, where the Pats were still playing, as a lucky charm of sorts. Fast forward to the 2002 Super Bowl, and they win. The two initially chalked it up to mere coincidence. That is, until the stadium was about to be demolished and Lou went and grabbed the nail, keeping it with him instead of finding a new hiding place. The result? Not even a spot in the 2002 season playoffs. Now officially committed to the power of the nail, Lou decided to see how well it worked in the new stadium. With the nail back where it belonged, the Patriots enjoyed an incredible run and won the Super Bowl in 2004.

Faced with undeniable proof that there was something incredible going on with this sharp little trinket, the men thought bigger, bolder. A different venue. A different sport. The nail found its way to Fenway Park for the Red Sox's 2004 season and, well...you know the rest.

So, where's the nail these days, you ask? Revealing the answer would ruin all of the fun of the search. Here's a potentially helpful hint: before you start looking, see which local sports team seems to be having the best luck at the moment. Happy hunting...and watch out for that sharp point.

Address Fenway Park, 4 Jersey Street, Boston, www.mlb.com/redsox/ballpark; TD Garden, 100 Legends Way, Boston, www.tdgarden.com; Gillette Stadium, 1 Patriot Place, Foxborough, www.gillettestadium.com | **Getting there** Varies | **Hours** See stadium websites | **Tip** Root, root, root for the home teams as you relive their most incredible victories and illustrious history at The Sports Museum inside the TD Garden (100 Legends Way, Boston, www.sportsmuseum.org).

75 The Mapparium
Journey to the center of the Earth

The Mapparium at the Christian Science Plaza is a giant, stained-glass globe of the world that you can walk through on a glass bridge, and it's one of the most unusual and colorful spaces in Boston.

The Mapparium offers a uniquely accurate perspective on the world – from the inside rather than the outside, as is typical of most globes. The shapes of the countries and continents are proportionally accurate here, as each part of the sphere is a different distance from your eye. There's no foreshortening that you'd see looking at the same shapes from the outside. You'll see that many geopolitical borders and names have changed since the Mapparium was completed in 1935, reflecting how ideas have traversed time and geography to transform the world. For example, the State of Israel did not yet exist.

Conceived by architect Chester Lindsay Churchill, the Mapparium remains a symbol for the global outreach of *The Christian Science Monitor* and a feature of The Christian Science Publishing Society's art deco building. The Mapparium was also Boston's answer to the spinning globe in the lobby of the *New York Daily News* Building in New York City. In this instance, Boston may have ended up with the more magnificent object in the Mapparium and its three stories' worth of elegant, richly colored, curved stained glass. In 2015, the lighting was updated to 175 computerized LED fixtures, providing a dramatic new brightness in the globe. In addition to the red, green, and blue colors of light used in the past, amber and white were also added. The Mapparium now glows even more vividly.

There is also a very special acoustic feature that you should try out. Because of the curvature of the space and the reflective qualities of the glass, this world keeps no secrets. Have a friend whisper something to you from one end of the walkway, and you will hear every word of it perfectly from the opposite end of the bridge.

Address 200 Massachusetts Avenue, Boston, MA 02115, +1 (617) 450-7000, www.marybakereddylibrary.org/project/mapparium, librarymail@mbelibrary.org | Getting there Subway to Prudential or Symphony (Green "E" Line) or Hynes Convention Center (Green "B," "C," or "D" Lines) | Hours Mon–Sat 10am–5pm, Sun 11am–5pm | Tip The Boston Symphony Orchestra has a range of family-friendly musical programming, and it's just a short walk from the library (301 Massachusetts Avenue, Boston, www.bso.org).

76 Marathon Bombing Memorial

Always in our hearts

April 15, 2013, 2:49 pm, a moment that changed the city forever. On a day that celebrates resilience, perseverance, and achievement every year, Boston was tested like never before when two bombs detonated near the Marathon finish line, killing Krystle Campbell, Lu Lingzi, and Martin Richard (see ch. 77), and injuring more than 260 others. During the ensuing manhunt and standoff, which kept city residents in fear for hours, two more lost their lives: MIT police officer Sean Collier and Boston police officer Dennis Simmonds.

The memorial, located at two different sites close to the race's finish line, took four years to plan and create. Gloucester-based sculptor Pablo Eduardo, who is behind other works around the city, like *St. Thomas More and Plazuela* at Boston College and the *Mayor Kevin White* statue in Faneuil Hall, constructed spires from bronze and glass at each memorial to represent the fragile nature of life. At night, light shines through the glass, creating a beautiful illuminating effect. The centerpieces of both are stone pillars that were gathered from places significant to each of the victims. Lingzi's stone was taken from the BU Bridge, where she attended school; Martin's was pulled from Franklin Park, his favorite place to play; and Krystle's comes from Spectacle Island, where she spent summers working at a snack bar.

At the bottom of the column of one site, an inscription: *All we have lost is brightly lost.* And the other: *Let us climb, now, the road to hope.* Two bronze bricks in the sidewalk are dedicated to each of the police officers. Eduardo worked closely with the victims' families as he designed the installation in order to honor their memories. Cherry trees planted between the spires bloom every April near the time of the tragedy as a reminder of the city's strength and solidarity.

Address 671 Boylston Street, Boston, MA 02116 | Getting there Subway to Copley (Green Line) or Back Bay (Orange Line) | Hours Unrestricted | Tip While you're in the area, you can't miss the legendary blue and yellow Boston Marathon finish line, where dreams quite literally come true for thousands of runners each year (678–652 Boylston Street, Boston).

77 Martin's Park

A playground with a purpose

The legacy of Martin Richard, the youngest victim of the Marathon bombing (see ch. 76), lives on through this beautiful, interactive park in the Seaport that opened in 2019. At just eight years old, Martin senselessly lost his life in 2013 in the terrorist attack, leaving behind his parents Bill and Denise, sister Jane, and brother Henry.

The park's location next to the Boston Children's Museum makes it the perfect outdoor complement to the indoor exhibits and an easy way to plan a whole day of family fun. Landscape architecture firm Michael Van Valkenburgh & Associates planned and designed the project, with extensive input from the Richard family.

Even the antsiest of little ones will be hard-pressed to get bored with all of the opportunities to use their imagination across the full acre of green space and structures designed with natural materials. There are telescopes that look out to Fort Point Channel, hills and ropes to climb, nature trails to explore, oversized baskets in which to swing, and even more enticements.

The large, two-level play ship is a major draw, adding a bit of nautical whimsy. A series of "talk tubes," a modern take on the old-school tin can telephone, emphasizes communication. On hot summer days, kids keep cool and splash around the water garden with fountains and mist that they can control themselves. On chillier days, the garden's boulders are the perfect location for games of tag. Parents and caretakers have plenty of options for respite too, with benches, seat walls, and viewpoints scattered throughout the park.

Martin's Park was built with accessibility for all ages in mind, so every visitor can enjoy what it has to offer, whether it's a three-level climbing structure or an embankment slide. All of it's made even lovelier with natural touches, including 350 trees and more than 4,000 white daffodils.

Address Next to the Boston Children's Museum, South Boston, MA 02210, +1 (617) 635-4500, www.bostonchildrensmuseum.org/martins-park | Getting there Subway to South Station (Red Line) or Courthouse (Silver Line) | Hours Daily dawn–dusk | Tip Also kid-friendly and boasting water views, thanks to its location on top of a floating barge(!), is the Boston Tea Party Ships & Museum (306 Congress Street, Boston, www.bostonteapartyship.com), where you can learn what was brewing during the city's most famous act of rebellion.

78_ The MCZ

You'll bug out over their beetles

The Harvard Museum of Natural History, often called "the MCZ" (Museum of Comparative Zoology) by locals, is the only place in Boston where you can fully satisfy your need to see taxidermized animals. Their collection includes hippos, zebras, lions, ostriches, hyena, gorillas, Siberian, Tasmanian and Indian tigers, cheetahs, jaguars, anteaters, sloths, buffalo, moose, giraffes, a giant armadillo, and a magnificent peacock with its tailfeathers spread wide. If you love taxidermy so much that you want to take it home, check the museum website for squirrel taxidermy workshops offered regularly in the spring and fall.

In addition to stuffed animals, the museum has skeletons of many long-extinct creatures, including one of the earliest Triceratops skulls ever found. It is world famous for its "glass flowers," hyper realistic models of 780 plant species made by a father and son team of Czech glass artists, Leopold and Rudolf Blaschka, at the turn of the 20th century. The Blaschka's glass sea creatures, which get a bit less attention, are equally elegant.

The Harvard Museum of Natural History also holds a special place in the hearts of bug lovers for its voluminous collection of iridescent beetles, gathered personally by none other than banker and philanthropist David Rockefeller. The collection, representing 90 years of bug hunting, includes over 150,000 specimens from around the world, the most glamorous of which are featured in the museums' exhibit, "Arthropods: Creatures That Rule." It's fascinating to see what pursuing one's childhood hobby all the way through to the end of one's life with no financial barriers looks like.

Admission to the museum includes access to the Peabody Museum of Archeology and Ethnology, which does basically everything that the MCZ does, except with a focus on people and human cultural history rather than the natural world.

Address 26 Oxford Street, Cambridge, MA 02138, +1 (617) 495-3045, www.hmnh.harvard.edu, hmnh@hmsc.harvard.edu | Getting there Subway to Harvard (Red Line) | Hours Daily 9am–5pm | Tip Harvard's Science Center Plaza (1 Oxford Street, Cambridge) has varying, year-round outdoor fun for everyone, including a fountain/sprinkler in the summer and a fire pit in the winter. Food trucks, beanbag games and an ice rink have also been known to pop up from time to time.

79__The Museum of Modern Renaissance

Magical mandalas in the middle of Somerville

Artists Nicholas Shaplyko and Ekaterina Sorokina, a pair of Russian transplants to the Boston area, have collaboratively converted a de-sanctified Morman temple into an intricate, dreamy, and ever-evolving act of art-worship. Their vision and their approach are like nothing else in the region. Here's how they explain it on their website: "We decided to make something different from today's art world, something like the Italian Renaissance. Then, art was a song of beauty about the human body, the human soul, human creativity, and human ability. It was the resurrection of a spirit that had been forgotten."

The two artists have worked together, painting fresco after fresco within and onto the outside of an incredible building that is both their home and a church-like sanctuary space. The couple doesn't discuss in advance what they'll paint but lets the works emerge from their shared impulses. They also have a strict color palette, using only what they call the seven pure tones, colors associated with the auras of the Hindu chakra system.

The results are intense and beautiful – swirling, pulsating patterns that feel like bright, woven tapestries or stained-glass windows. Peppered with birds, animals and mythical creatures, the paintings feel magical. The museum is apparently located in the very spot where yoga was first introduced to the United States. In 1920, the building was a Unitarian Church that hosted Paramahansa Yogananda, who gave a presentation on the philosophy of Yoga.

The museum is Shaplyko and Sorokina's private home, so visiting the inside requires an appointment, but it's also worth appreciating from the outside. And keep an eye on their website, as they occasionally host art openings and concerts, which are usually also quite unique.

Address 115 College Avenue, Somerville, MA 02144, www.mod-renaissance.com, museum@mod-ren.com | Getting there Subway to Davis (Red Line) | Hours Unrestricted from the outside, call for appointment to enter | Tip Before making the pilgrimage to this museum, grab a cup of some of the best coffee in town at Diesel Cafe (257 Elm Street, Somerville, www.diesel-cafe.com). It's impossible to find a seat there, so get a to-go cup for your walk up College Avenue.

80 NETA

Greenbacks to green buds

When former Brookline residents who used to bank at the main branch of Brookline Savings Bank in Brookline Village come back to town for a first visit in a long time, they will be very surprised to find that their neighborhood institution is not the one they once knew. It doles out a different kind of green nowadays – to lines around the block.

This incredibly ornate bank with giant antique vault doors and a stained-glass domed ceiling always looked more like a place of worship than a place to apply for a loan, and now it is somewhat more of a mix between business and pleasure. NETA, the first recreational marijuana store to open up in the Boston area, has replaced tables full of deposit and withdrawal slips with display cases full of golden distillates, glazed shatter, powdery kief, chunky yellow waxes, and ripe green buds. Instead of jewels, their safe deposit boxes now contain colorful edibles: gummies, chocolates, cubes, chews, cooking oils… And tellers are replaced with advisors, who can help you decide which THC-laced tinctures, lotions, and even suppositories are likely to cure what ails you.

NETA grows the strains it sells locally and makes many of the products on display themselves. Their staff are knowledgeable, understanding and enthusiastic about the benefits of weed. And as mentioned previously, the shop itself is drop dead gorgeous – there is no more elegant place in town to make your THC and CBD purchases.

Unless you go during off hours or have a medical marijuana card, you should expect long lines. You'll want to browse and ask questions the first time you go, but once you know what you like, you can order online and just pick up with ID. But if you have the time, go in and poke around to see what's new. If there's a new cannabis trend or technology out there, they'll be showcasing it. You can bank on it.

Address 160 Washington Street, Brookline, MA 02445, +1 (617) 841-7250, www.netacare.org/brookline, contact@netacare.org | Getting there Subway to Brookline Village (Green "D" Line) | Hours For recreational shopping: Mon–Sat 10am–7:45pm, Sun noon–5:45pm | Tip Chances are, er, high that you're going to get hungry after you visit NETA. Pick up a hearty sandwich from Cutty's (284 Washington Street, Brookline, www.cuttyfoods.com) before you partake responsibly.

81 November Project

Cheapest gym membership ever

It's possible they're bonkers. They get up at 5am in the middle of frigid Boston winters and make their individual ways to different places around the city that they get notified about a few days before. And then they flash mob their way through an intensive workout – together, but each at their own pace. All before work.

It's also possible they're smart. In a city where a gym membership can cost upwards of $150/month, and some personal trainers cost about that much per hour, a system that motivates people to gather regularly and work out intensively a few times a week, using nothing but the city's unique public and private architectural features as work-out equipment, is not at all a bad idea.

What they unquestionably are is contagious. Though the November Project was started in Boston by two friends motivating each other to run outdoors when chilly November rolled around, it now has chapters around the world. But you don't have to be training for the Boston Marathon to run with this pack. All you have to do is show up and do your best workout.

At the beginning, the group ran up and down the bleachers of Harvard's large football stadium three times a week, but now it roams to different locations depending on the day. On Monday, they mix it up, but the Boston Landing Track & Field in Brighton is a good bet. Wednesday, they usually revisit Harvard's Stadium. On Friday, they run up Summit Avenue on the Brighton/Brookline line. But it's all subject to change, so you'll need to sign up on their website for their weekly invites.

You can join in once or make it a decade-long habit. In either case, you'll find a welcoming community of cheerleaders to get you through the brutality of the workout that they promise is accessible to everyone, even couch potatoes. See for yourself if that's true.

Address Various, sign up at www.november-project.com/boston for weekly invites | Getting there Varies | Hours Mon & Fri 6:30am, Wed 5:30am & 6:30am | Tip On days when the group meets near Boston Landing, grab some top-of-the-line gear at the New Balance Global Flagship store (140 Guest Street, Boston, stores.newbalance.com/globalflagshipbostonlanding), an immersive, 6,566-square-foot retail experience that features demonstration and shoe assembly areas.

82 Nuggets

Digging for gold and platinum

A funky record store like Nuggets might seem slightly out of place in the sports-centric neighborhood of Kenmore Square, but it's a local institution that's almost as storied as Fenway Park. In fact, owner Stuart Freedman has a long history with the shop that dates back to the late 1970s. It all started as a labor of love, with three guys hawking vinyl out of cardboard boxes on the sidewalk until they saved up enough to purchase their own storefront. Freedman joined the staff while he was still a college student at Northeastern, and the rest, of course, was hi-fi history.

While many things in the world – and Boston – have changed in four decades, it's comforting to know that this spot hasn't. Walking into the store is like stepping back in time in the absolute best way, with stacks and stacks as far as the eye can see, no frills to be found, and an insane amount of music knowledge. From Fleetwood Mac to Fugazi, folk to freakbeat, you'll find every genre under the sun and then some, though good ol' classic rock still reigns supreme. True to its name, Nuggets specializes in rare, out-of-print, and unusual records, so don't be shy about asking the staff if they can work some magic to snag a limited release for you.

Though it's a browser's paradise that lends itself to sorting for hours, marveling at some of the truly inspired cover art, rest assured that everything is completely alphabetized. So if you're in the market for something specific, it shouldn't take you too long to track it down. It's not just vinyl, either; you'll find cassettes, videos, posters, and even CDs – remember those? To be certain, Nuggets is of an earlier era, and while many of its kind have expanded their online presence, everything here is decidedly brick-and-mortar. If you're dying to get those AC/DC LPs from the 1980s off of your hands, the shop does a solid buying and trading business as well.

Address 486 Commonwealth Avenue, Boston, MA 02215, +1 (617) 536-0679, www.nuggetsrecords.com | **Getting there** Subway to Kenmore Square (Green "B," "C," or "D" Lines) | **Hours** Tue–Sat 11:30am–7pm, Sun noon–5pm | **Tip** Shop for even more pop culture down the street at Comicopia (464 Commonwealth Avenue, Boston, www.comicopia.com), a longstanding purveyor of graphic novels.

83___Olives & Grace
Great gifts for good

You won't find any tacky tourist t-shirts here. Olives & Grace is a South End gift shop, far away – both literally and figuratively – from the lobster bibs and Sox caps of Faneuil Hall, that sources all of its products from small businesses and local artisans. Owner Sofi Madison started the boutique in 2012 as "a curtsy to the makers," which is also the store's tagline. The boutique is small in size but big in heart, generosity, and substance.

The shelves are stocked with a perfect balance of cozy and cheeky: think Ruth Bader Ginsberg prayer candles, ceramic mugs, floral sleep masks, and even organic cocktail syrups. The common thread is that they're all thoughtfully handpicked. Behind each is a story of creativity and passion that can be felt in every handmade necklace and tea towel. New inventory arrives at the store just about every day, and much of the merchandise incorporates natural, regional ingredients.

At Olives & Grace, it's as much about engaging with the community as it is about offering one-of-a-kind items. For example, one of the vendors is a social enterprise that partners with artisan groups around the world to ensure sustainable jobs for women. Another uses profits from their tea sales to educate young orphans in Kenyan villages.

The store also hosts events that not only showcase its selection of food and drink offerings – from olive oil and honey to caramels – but also allow shoppers to chat with and learn from the makers themselves. Tarot card readings, floral arrangement workshops, and calligraphy lessons bring the products to life too.

Really want to take your gift game to the next level? Tap into the staff's expertise and add a personal touch to your present by custom-curating a box of goodies for your friend, family member, or better half. Choose from themes like Boston, ceramics, specialty foods, and apothecary supplies.

Address 623 Tremont Street, Boston, MA 02118, +1 (617) 236-4536, www.olivesandgrace.com, info@olivesandgrace.com | Getting there Subway to Back Bay (Orange Line) | **Hours** Tue–Sat 11am–7pm, Sun 11am–5pm | Tip Not ready to end your gift shopping spree yet? Pop into SAULT (577 Tremont Street, Boston, www.saultne.com) to pick up a few rugged accessories and guy-approved grooming products for the dude in your life.

84 Omni Parker House

John, Jackie, and Ho Chi Minh walk into a hotel

The 551-room Omni Parker House luxury hotel is an elegant, ornate piece of living history. Its wood-paneled walls and floral carpets have witnessed the daily doings of everyone from Nathaniel Hawthorne to Emeril Lagasse, and a few ghosts to boot.

One wonders what John Wilkes Booth, who stayed here about a week before assassinating Abraham Lincoln, thought of the hotel's strange coat of arms: a mashup including a pineapple, a deer's head, a Scottish terrier, a horse (or maybe it's a goat?) and a hand holding an olive branch. One could wonder the same of Ralph Waldo Emerson, Henry Wadsworth Longfellow, Henry David Thoreau, or even Charles Dickens, who all shared their work here at a renowned literary salon that the hotel once hosted.

A curiosity not on public view is a medieval-looking device called a Dutchess dough divider, used in the kitchen to section one piece of dough into 36 smaller ones instantly. It's been in operation here since at least 1911, when Ho Chi Minh used it to make the Omni's restaurant's famous Parker House Rolls. Did this culinary beast inspire his political theories? Or those of Malcom X, who also did a stint on the hotel's staff? Chefs Emeril Lagasse, Lydia Shire, and Jasper White also rotated through the hotel's kitchen, which is also where the Boston cream pie was invented.

The restaurant's fine ambience and food are probably why John F. Kennedy is rumored to have brought Jacqueline Bouvier here to propose. How could she say "no" at the corner table, surrounded by the Omni's red velvet curtains and sparkling chandeliers?

Not impressed by the hotel's famous visitors? Maybe you will be by its more infamous ones. Many ghost sightings have been reported, including hotel's founder Harvey Parker, who checks on his 10th floor guests on occasion.

Address 60 School Street, Boston, MA 02108, +1 (617) 227-8600, www.omnihotels.com/hotels/boston-parker-house | Getting there Subway to Park Street (Red or Green Line) or Government Center (Green or Blue Line) | Hours See website for restaurant hours | Tip Have an old-school, ultra romantic dinner at JFK's table at the Omni, and then go rock out at the Orpheum, one of the oldest theaters in the country. Or vice versa (1 Hamilton Place, Boston, www.crossroadspresents.com/pages/orpheum-theatre).

85 Overlook Shelter Ruins

Puddin' on the ritz

In addition to deserted zoo exhibits (see ch. 47), Franklin Park is also home to remnants of one of the earliest examples of Frederick Law Olmsted's influential architecture. If the name doesn't ring a bell, his most well-known project, Manhattan's Central Park, might. The park is one of nine connected expanses designed by Olmsted that comprise a chain called The Emerald Necklace (see ch. 105). No offense to Jamaica Pond or The Arboretum, but with its historic detail and stunning scenery, Franklin is widely considered to be the "crown jewel" of the entire bunch.

The primary building, a two-story structure, was used for multiple purposes throughout the early 1900s, including a police station and a field house and viewing spot for athletic events. Fortunately, that vantage point remains unchanged, making it easy to picture races, games, and matches taking place below. Today, there's also a permanent dedicated sports venue, White Stadium, that opened in 1949.

Due to a fire in 1945 that completely incinerated that main building, the site lost a bit of its former glory. Fortunately, it was given a second life in the 1960s by a local activist. Elma Lewis created a popular outdoor concert venue at the ruins called Playhouse in the Park that drew locals to see big name stars, including Duke Ellington and Odetta. The tradition continues to this day with R&B, gospel, and reggae artists gracing the stage on summer evenings and children's programming during the day.

Crafted from the conglomerate rock puddingstone, a material that was extremely popular in the area at the time, the ruins also include a water fountain, an archway, benches, and steps that add a positively romantic and storybook quality to the setting. With a picnic lunch and maybe a parasol if you're feeling fancy, it's not hard to imagine yourself laughing and lounging amongst the 20th-century bourgeois.

Address Pier Point Road, Roxbury, MA 02121, +1 (617) 635-4505, www.boston.gov/parks/franklin-park | Getting there Subway to Stony Brook (Orange Line) | Hours Daily dawn–dusk | Tip For that picnic, grab some fresh empanadas and smoothies at PikaloX (3160 Washington Street, Boston, www.pikalox.com) and enjoy your leisurely lunch in the park.

86 The Paramount
Sit down for a killer brunch

Serving up toast with a side of true crime, The Paramount restaurant sits below the apartment where the Boston Strangler's final victim was discovered in 1964. On January 4 of that year, 19-year-old Mary Sullivan was found strangled with her own stocking, an eerie "Happy New Year" card at her feet. She had just moved in four days prior.

The strangler had been terrifying city residents for more than two years, with 13 victims, several suspects, and no answers. The women whose lives were tragically cut short ranged widely in age, the eldest being 85. In fact, the killer's original nickname was "the Mother Killer," due to his predilection for older victims. However, when two young women were found, a much more frightening picture emerged. Some even speculated that this was the work of more than one person.

In 1965, a mental hospital resident with a burglary record named Albert DeSalvo came forward to confess to the murders, but there was lingering doubt due to the nature of the crimes. To complicate matters, DeSalvo was murdered in prison in 1973, raising uncertainty as to whether the killings would ever be solved. That is, until 2013, when police found a DNA match between Mary Sullivan and one of DeSalvo's nephews. To confirm, the alleged killer's body was exhumed. After years of grief and fear, it was finally over. They had their guy, nearly 50 years later.

Through it all, The Paramount was a constant. The lively neighborhood joint has been doling out comfort food to Bostonians since 1937 via a cafeteria-style system that somehow always guarantees you a table once you get through the line, no matter how packed it is. Breakfast is the star of the show, with omelets, buttermilk pancakes, brioche French toast, and malted Belgian waffles. But you can also grab a mean reuben or eggplant parmigiana if hunger strikes at lunch or dinner time.

Address 44 Charles Street, Boston, MA 02114, +1 (617) 720-1152, www.paramountboston.com | Getting there Subway to Charles/MGH (Red Line) | Hours See website | Tip The Charles Street Meeting House at 70 Charles Street was a critical venue during the anti-slavery movement, hosting William Lloyd Garrison, Sojourner Truth, Harriet Tubman, and Frederick Douglass.

87_ The People's Karaoke
Sing it to me one more time

Karaoke. You either love it or you're being forced to do it at the socio-cultural equivalent of gunpoint by your coworkers or someone in your life who has a very different idea of what makes for a fun birthday than you do. Regardless, if you're going to do karaoke in Boston, it should be this karaoke because it's run by a pro. His name is Sparky.

The People's Karaoke is the best Karaoke in town, but it roves. Catch it Tuesday in Harvard Square, Wednesday in the South End, Thursday in Somerville, Friday in Kendall Square, Sunday in Fenway. You'll find a whole different scene at each location. Regulars and wild cards show up for each venue's edition, plus dedicated followers who follow Sparky from venue to venue as if he were the Grateful Dead – which you can sing if you want to, by the way.

The People's Karaoke has seven Grateful Dead songs in its voluminous songbook. And eight Judy Garland songs, 19 Marvin Gaye songs, two Ariana Grande songs, two Grandmaster Flash songs, and way too many Green Day songs. That's one half-page of their song list from bands with names starting with G. They also have songs by bands whose names begin with the other letters of the English alphabet and songs in Spanish, Swedish, French, German, Korean, Italian, and Japanese. Choose from a big selection of specialty songs, including ones celebrating major holidays, Broadway musicals, Irish drinking songs (highly recommended, even if you don't know them), and songs from Disney movies (a good time to go to the bathroom).

In addition to the kind of people who sing karaoke occasionally to celebrate something, or regularly to blow off steam, The People's Karaoke attracts dedicated karaoke-ists who treat the activity like a sport. Look out for groups in matching satin jackets with their own wireless mics because it happens occasionally, and when it does, you're in for a harmonic treat.

Address Various, www.thepeopleskaraoke.com | **Getting there** See website for locations | **Hours** See website for hours and venues | **Tip** If you can't get enough karaoke, get one last late-night or private group round in at Chinatown's Station KTV (20 Hudson Street, Boston, www.stationktv.com).

88 Polly Thayer Self-Portrait
A painter in her own strokes

The renowned Boston Athenaeum houses a number of incredible pieces of literature and art, including more than a handful by Polly Thayer Starr, one of the city's most unsung painters.

Born to Harvard Law School Dean Ezra Ripley Thayer and Ethel Randolph Thayer, and granddaughter of prominent scholar James Bradley Thayer, Polly was raised in the city.

She studied various forms of art at the School of the Museum of Fine Arts, including painting with Leslie Prince Thompson and figure drawing with Phillip L. Hale, with whom she eventually studied privately instead of continuing her studies at the school.

Her first solo exhibition took place in 1930 at the Doll and Richards Gallery. It was a major turning point in her career, garnering her 18 commissions as a result. Her art spanned a fairly wide range of subjects and themes, from flowers and animals to her own husband, Donald Starr. A devout Quaker from 1942 on, Thayer Starr's work became heavily influenced by her beliefs during this period. This oil on canvas created in 1943 is perhaps the most memorable, straightforward, and revealing of her self-portraits. It came to the Athenaeum in 1995, a gift of the artist herself.

It depicts Thayer Starr in a colorful outfit, with a dusty rose cap, matching scarf, a stylish wide-cuffed gauntlet glove on her right hand, and a piece of coral wrapped around her left fingers. Curator Dorothy Koval, who worked directly with the artist, explained that an earlier, smaller version of the work featured a paintbrush in her right hand instead. In both paintings, these touches gave small yet powerful glimpses into her personality, along with an undeniable twinkle in her eye. The painting's just one of the Athenaeum's six pieces by Thayer Starr, which include four portraits of others and one landscape piece. She died at age 102 in 2006, but her legacy lives on here.

Address 10 1/2 Beacon Street, Boston, MA 02108, +1 (617) 227-0270,
www.bostonathenaeum.org | Getting there Subway to Park Street (Red or Green Line)
or Government Center (Green or Blue Line) | Hours Mon–Thu 9am–8pm, Fri & Sat
9am–5pm | Tip On your way to the Athenaeum, stop in front of the State House to see
the Anne Hutchinson Statue and learn another little-known story about one of
America's first feminists (24 Beacon Street, Boston).

89 Porchfest

All the burb's a stage

Quoth Madonna in 2000, "Music makes the people come together." Madge is one wise woman, and Porchfest, a decentralized festival celebrating the beauty of community and sound, is perhaps the best example of this phenomenon. While the original event can be traced back to Ithaca, New York in 2007, the Boston area's first iteration took place in Somerville in 2011. Now, the annually-anticipated gathering, sponsored by local arts councils, has expanded to Jamaica Plain, Brookline, Arlington, Newton, and more. Each town or region offers its own unique take on porch plucking, playing, and percussing on a different weekend afternoon during the spring, summer, and fall, so true "porchheads" have the chance to attend them all.

The real beauty of Porchfest is its wildly diverse lineup, which spans genres from folk to hip-hop, to punk, and to heavy metal, showcasing everyone from veteran cover bands to housemates who decided to make some noise with guitars and banjos for an afternoon. You might even stumble upon some unexpected instruments. Somerville musician Jon Bernhardt draws a crowd year after year as he shows off his theremin skills with covers of The Ramones and Pixies. Don't know what a theremin is? Exactly.

With a rolling schedule that assigns a two-hour block of time to a designated section of streets, revelers can stroll (or bike, skateboard, or scoot) from porch to porch at a leisurely pace, enjoying the talents of local troubadours, making new friends, and catching up with old ones. As a result, the energy in the air is palpable, like a huge block party and concert all rolled into one. And much like a block party, food and drink are plentiful. Many generous hosts not only lend their porches to musicians for the day, but they'll also fire up their grills and tap their kegs for visitors to enjoy – or they'll at least offer some primo snacks to keep everyone's toes tapping.

Address Various, www.porchfest.info | **Getting there** Various locations | **Hours** See website for event schedule | **Tip** Get your live music fix all year round at The Sinclair (52 Church Street, Cambridge, www.sinclaircambridge.com), a small venue where indie rock reigns and there's not a bad view in the house.

90 Puppet Free Library
Come in and play

A hidden tribute to the lost art of puppetry sits in a similarly forgotten spot: the basement of Emmanuel Church. You can only get inside by going through an *Alice-in-Wonderland*-like door in a small alley. In fact, its original name was the Back Alley Puppet Theater, and it has remained one of the city's best-kept secrets for decades. Sara Peattie, a Chicago-born puppeteer, who trained and performed with the politically-inclined Bread and Puppet Theater Group, is the wildly creative and talented woman behind it all.

"The Puppet Free Library lies at the intersection of a random assortment of giant puppets and an even more random assortment of humans," she explains. "That's what I love about it."

It started in 1976, when Peattie and her husband formed a group called the Puppeteers' Cooperative and built several puppets for the city's inaugural First Night New Year's Eve celebration. Over the next 10 years, the practice of borrowing puppets continued informally, but a process of signing them in and out soon became routine.

These days, the library is a whimsical, one-stop shop for anyone looking to liven up their parade or community event with a little old-school magic (Somerville's annual HONK! Fest regularly shows off many of the library's beautiful pieces), or just add some fun to the day by marveling at Peattie's handiwork; it doubles as a studio for her.

As you wander through this large, colorful closet, you'll find your average-sized animal masks and delicate papier-mâché marionettes. But the real draws are the larger-than-life creations that are nothing short of spectacular, from 20-foot-tall "Mother Earth" masterpieces to footlong dancing cats, fiery dragons, and massive flowers.

In 2019, filmmaker Jared Leong created an eponymous five-minute documentary that details the history of the library and Peattie's story in exquisite detail – it's available to view for free on Vimeo.

Address 15 Public Alley, No. 437, Boston, MA 02116, +1 (617) 263-2031, www.puppetco-op.org/libraries.htm, puppetco@puppetco-op.org | Getting there Subway to Arlington (Green Line) | Hours Tue – Sat 2 – 7pm, or by appointment | Tip Can't get enough of this quirky art form? Enjoy one of the creative, family-friendly performances at the Puppet Showplace Theater (32 Station Street, Brookline, www.puppetshowplace.org).

91   Rebel Rebel

Where every night is ladies' night

With natural wine aplenty and a namesake pulled from a Bowie song, Rebel Rebel epitomizes elevated cool. Oh, and did we mention that it's completely woman owned and operated? In 2018, Lauren Friel set up shop in Somerville's Bow Market, a collection of local retail and food businesses in Union Square. The bar's compact size – just 20 seats inside – seems expressly designed to encourage close conversations with bartenders and fellow patrons. This is all part of its charm. In warm weather, you can sit and sip *al fresco* on the stone patio.

Unlike many bars that attempt to do it all, Rebel Rebel focuses on the thing they do really, really well: wine that's free of additives and carefully procured from family vineyards and female winemakers. An intentionally minimal and curated snack menu includes a cheese tray from Formaggio Kitchen (see ch. 46), olives, and potato chips fried in oil and shipped in from Spain.

A veteran of the Boston food and wine scene, Friel was named *Boston* magazine's Sommelier of the Year in 2019, has served as Wine Director for Oleana and Sarma, and wrote wine programs for Committee, The Wine Bottega, and other local hotspots. As a consultant, she also created the country's only all-female wine list for Dirt Candy in New York. She and the staff share their abundance of beverage knowledge with regular classes that focus on vino varieties from a particular region and individual winemakers.

Rebel Rebel is more than just a place to drink wine; it's an attitude. The room is illuminated with pink lighting, and the wall is emblazoned with the mantra "SEX MONEY POWER." Instead of a tip jar, the bar features a "Donate to Planned Parenthood" jar. Its website instructs you to "Leave your misogyny, your homophobia, your racism, your classism, your ableism, your patriarchy, your gender bias, and all your other bullshit at the door."

Address 1 Bow Market Way, Somerville, MA 02143, www.rebelrebelsomerville.com | Getting there Bus 85 or 87 to Somerville Avenue at Union Square; bus 91 or CT 2 to Somerville Avenue & Stone Avenue | Hours Mon–Fri 4pm–midnight, Sat & Sun noon–midnight | Tip One perk of being in the middle of Bow Market: you can grab food from one spot and bring it into another to eat! Try some empanadas from Buenas, clam chowder from Hooked, or poutine from Saus. Better yet, try all three (www.bowmarketsomerville.com).

92 Revere's Piping Plovers

Winged friends at America's oldest public beach

Revere is the oldest public beach in the United States, and it's a decidedly urban one. There's no way around the fact that it's on Logan Airport's flight path. But what it lacks in bucolic charms, it makes up for in liveliness and giant, sun-bleached quahog shells.

Revere is changing quickly. By the time you read this, the huge, new apartment buildings overlooking Revere Beach will be finished, and there will be more joggers and strollers along Ocean Avenue than there ever have been. That's saying a lot, as Revere, named after Paul Revere, has been the first point of entry for wave after wave of immigrants since the 1620s. English settlers were followed by waves of Irish, German, and Italian immigrants, and then Russian and Polish Jews flooded the city for the first few decades of the 20th century. The most recent waves are from Morocco and Brazil. Overall, the city's population is more than 25% foreign-born.

So it goes without saying that Revere Beach is a diverse and interesting place to plop down a towel and beach umbrella and people-watch on a hot summer's day.

The beach hosts a surprising number of piping plover nests. Any beach you visit along the Massachusetts coastline will have a protected area set aside for piping plover breeding, but it feels somehow especially wonderous to see these little white puffball sea birds hopping and swooping around in large numbers on Revere Beach. Like Revere's many other immigrants, the tiny, endangered plovers have come a long way – often as far away as Mexico, without stopping – with hopes of finding a safe place to raise their families.

Despite the bustle of the boulevard, the Plovers fit in. They've been coming for a long time, and when you see these little puffs perched up in the rafters of Revere Beach's antique shade shelters, it's too easy just to hope they'll thrive here.

DO NOT ENTER

This is a breeding area for Plovers, Terns, Skimmers and Oyster Catchers

LEAST TERN   PIPING PLOVER

**THESE BREEDING BIRDS,
THEIR NESTS AND EGGS
ARE PROTECTED**

UNDER FEDERAL LAW (16 U.S.C. 703)

Persons May Be Arrested and Fined for Killing,
Harassing or in Any Way Disturbing These Birds

Address 600 Ocean Avenue, Revere, MA 02151, www.reverebeach.com | Getting there Subway to Wonderland (Blue Line). Cross the tiny suspension bridge outside of the top level of the station to the beach. | Hours See website for beach hours and conditions | Tip Once a year, usually in mid-July, Revere beach hosts a multi-day, international sand sculpting festival. People come from all over the world to sculpt sandcastles competitively, and over a million people come to cheer them on (Revere Beach, Revere, www.internationalsandsculptingfestival.com).

93 Sacco's Bowl Haven

Pies and pins

Pizza: great. Bowling: also great. The combination of pizza *and* bowling? Now we're talking. The low-key, old-school vibe at Sacco's lends itself to a Sunday afternoon family outing as well as it does to a weeknight date or a way to keep boredom at bay with a handful of your closest pals. The alley is equal parts 1970s-infused, *Dazed and Confused* hangout and uplifting casual eatery, the walls bearing phrases like "Keep each other well," and "Think good thoughts." Fully committed to the retro theme, they still score using paper and a pencil.

And because this is New England, the tradition of candlepin bowling remains alive and well. For the unfamiliar or uninitiated, the style originated in Worcester, Massachusetts in the 1880s and incorporates narrow pins that resemble candles and handheld balls without finger holes. There are other subtle differences that set it apart too, like rolling three balls per frame instead of two, and having to navigate around the fallen pins in between rolls, since they're not cleared away until the end of the frame.

Given the added degree of difficulty, you just might need some liquid courage before facing down the pins. Fortunately, Sacco's boasts a full bar, and you can even have a beer or cocktail delivered right to your lane along with your pizza in case you need to nurse your sorrows right then and there. Now that's service!

Speaking of which, you might be surprised to find out that the flatbreads here are pretty fancy for a bowling alley. They're wood-fired in clay ovens, and they feature a variety of toppings that include free-range pork and chicken, artisan cheese, organic mushrooms, and garlic oil that's made in-house. Homemade, classic desserts are also on the menu: think brownie sundaes, root beer floats, and whoopie pies. Tuesday night is Benefit Night, where portions of the proceeds from all flatbreads sold go to a different local nonprofit.

Address 45 Day Street, No. 2823, Somerville, MA 02144, +1 (617) 776-0552, www.saccobowl.com | Getting there Subway to Davis (Red Line) | Hours Sun–Wed 10am–10pm, Thu–Sat 10am–midnight | Tip When in Davis Square for the evening, stop for a pint at The Burren (247 Elm Street, Somerville, www.burren.com), a pub where Irish musicians fiddle away next to neighborhood elders, college kids, and everyone in between.

94 Sacred Cod

Thank cod for small favors

This is probably the most bizarre artifact in Boston. It's not so much that it's a hyper realistic, almost five-foot long codfish hanging in the House Chamber in the Massachusetts State House (though that is pretty weird, right?), but that it's there to make sure that public servants never forget the critical importance of cod fishery.

The current cod, which has been the official cod since 1784, once had to be moved from one part of the State House to another, and it was wrapped in an American flag and carried like a coffin by house messengers and escorted by the state's Sergeant-at-Arms while making this short journey – a method decided upon by House vote after the three-member Committee on History of the Emblem of the Codfish presented the recommendation. This cod replaces a similar cod that is believed to have been stolen and destroyed in 1773 by a British trooper during the Siege of Boston. It had in turn replaced the original cod, which perished when the original State House burned down in 1747. The origin of this ur-cod is unknown.

What is known is that the cod fish is deeply important to the State of Massachusetts. Cod fishing was the first colonial industry and supposedly the first export. From a symbolic perspective, according to *A History of the Emblem of the Codfish in the Hall of the House of Representatives* that was compiled by the House Committee to decide about the cod's transit within the State House in 1895, the cod represents the state: "It commemorates Democracy. It celebrates the rise of free institutions. It emphasizes progress. It epitomizes Massachusetts."

The cod made national headlines when it was "cod-napped" in 1933 by members of the Harvard Lampoon (see ch. 57). They smuggled their prize out of the building disguised in an oversized box of flowers. The police dragged the Charles River searching for it before it was ultimately returned.

Address 24 Beacon Street, Boston, MA 02133, +1 (617) 727-3676, www.malegislature.gov/ StateHouse/Tour | Getting there Subway to Park Street (Red or Green Line), to Downtown Crossing (Red or Orange Line), or Government Center (Green or Blue Line) | Hours Free walking tours Mon–Fri 10am–3:30pm | Tip Head to the New England Aquarium's "Gulf of Maine" exhibit (1 Central Wharf, Boston, www.neaq.org/exhibit/gulf-of-maine) to find several of the less sacred, great, great, great, great grandfish of whichever cod modeled for the sculpture in the State House.

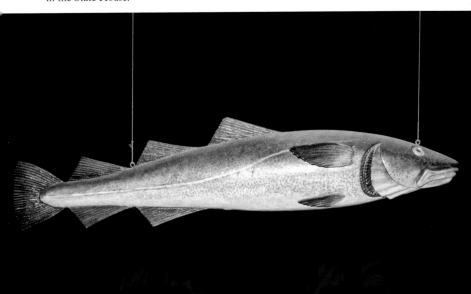

95 _ Salmagundi
A haven for hats

The right hat can take any look to the next level, and Jamaica Plain's Salmagundi has 12,000 to choose from, for both "ladies and gents." Harkening back to the days when fashion was a bit more dapper, the boutique might initially appear to be straight out of a bygone era with all of its fiddler caps, derbies, and cloches. But it actually opened its doors in 2007. True to its name, which means "a miscellaneous collection," there's just about every type of headwear you can imagine.

However, the method of husband-and-wife team Andria Rapagnola and Jessen Fitzpatrick still remains deeply rooted in the traditions of yore, like working with area hatmakers – or milliners, if you want to be fancy about it – to craft customized pieces that will help you stand out in a crowd. In addition, the staff take a personalized approach to helping you find the perfect bowler or beret that works with your face shape and fits you both literally and style-wise. Plus, visitors to the showroom are encouraged to have fun and try on hats to their hearts' content. Even if you don't consider yourself "a hat person," you might just change your mind after stepping into this special shop and seeing all the choices.

It's not all about new purchases, either. Not only are there a variety of hat care products to keep your topper in tip-top shape (and you looking like a million bucks), but the shop is home to a complete hat restoration workshop that offers services, such as custom trims, repairs, blocking, and cleaning.

A small and curated selection of handbags, ties, belts, gloves, and even flasks will help you pull it all together and dress to impress at your next roaring 1920s party. Or your next trip to the grocery store — you'll look fabulous wherever you go. This location is the original Salmagundi, but there's a smaller outpost in the North End that can also satisfy your need for a classy finishing touch on your outfit.

Address 765 Centre Street, Jamaica Plain, MA 02130, +1 (617) 522-5047, www.salmagundiboston.com, order@salmagundiboston.com | Getting there Subway to Green Street (Orange Line) | Hours Wed–Sat 11am–5pm | Tip Don your new old-fashioned hat and take a tour of the Loring Greenough House (12 South Street, Jamaica Plain, www.loring-greenough.org), the last remaining residence from the 18th century in JP's Sumner Hill neighborhood.

96 The Sargent Gallery
It took nearly 30 years and still isn't done

Painter John Singer Sargent (1856–1925) was born in Europe, but he had Boston area roots, as his father was from Gloucester, MA. Unlike many artists, Sargent was quite famous in his lifetime, commanding prices that were the days' equivalent of over $100,000 for commissions of his luminous portraits. Though most known now for these, and for his landscapes, all of which hang in private or museum collections, his most significant accomplishment as a painter is installed at the main branch of the Boston Public Library, free for all to spend time with during the library's opening hours.

Sargent's enormous mural *Triumph of Religion* runs along all four walls and across the vaulted ceilings of the library's skylight-filled Sargent Gallery. Sargent had been given free reign to paint on any subject that interested him, and the mural was intended to highlight important moments in the history of early Egyptian and Assyrian religion, Judaism and Christianity, based on his self-study of the subjects. Sargent painted the mural panels in his London studio, transported them to Boston, and mounted them, along with much custom gilded molding meant to lend a sense of the sacred to their arrangement, over the course of 29 years.

Each of the 19 mural panels represents a specific theme, for example "pagan gods," "hell," or "the passing of souls into heaven." There were supposed to be 20 panels, but one – depicting Jesus' sermon on the mount – was never completed, so the central panel in the gallery remains empty. The mural was never finished because of a controversy it raised. Boston's Jewish community felt Sargent's depiction of "the synagogue" was insensitive. Then Sargent got derailed from the project by a death in his family and a commission from Boston's Museum of Fine Arts while the controversy played out. He had a heart attack and died before he could return to the project.

Address 700 Boylston Street, Boston, MA 02116, +1 (617) 536.5400, www.bpl.org/ mckim-points-of-interest/#sargent, ask@bpl.org | Getting there Subway to Copley (Green Line) or Back Bay (Orange Line) | Hours Mon–Thu 9am–9pm, Fri & Sat 9am–5pm, Sun 1–5pm | Tip In London, Sargent shared an enormous studio space with Austin Abbey, who was working on a mural for the library as well. Go see it too in the library's Abbey Room (www.bpl.org/mckim-points-of-interest/#abbey).

97 _ Singing Beach

The sand is alive with the sound of music

On a hot day in Boston, you will want to take advantage of the city's proximity to the ocean and its robust commuter rail system. Most of Boston's beaches that are easily accessible by public transportation are pretty urban. But there is a really beautiful public beach about a 10-minute walk from the Manchester-by-the-Sea commuter rail stop on what Bostonians call "the North Shore." It's named Singing Beach for the whistling of its dunes and the noticeably loud squeaks you make with each step when you walk on its gleaming white sands.

Only about a half a mile long but stunning, Singing Beach has all of the essential beach amenities – a changing room built in the 1920s and a tiny snack shop run by locals – but not much else. And it's perfect. It gets crowded on weekends as all beaches do, but a weekday visit at midday on any but the hottest days of the year will leave you with enough personal space and privacy for quiet beach lounging or an uninterrupted stroll along one of the rocky outcroppings at either end of the beach. Gaze off contemplatively at several small islands (Rock Dundy, Salt Rock, and Little Salt Rocks) off in the distance, brave the usually cold waters as New Englanders do every summer, or just walk the shoreline squeakily while your body takes in the vitamin D it was starving for all winter.

A few caveats: if you bring a picnic or hit the snack bar, be alert to the seagulls here. They are beyond bold, and they gang up – they're fully capable of extracting a whole hot dog, bun and all, from your hand while you're still standing at the snack kiosk, topping it with mustard. Also, don't try to drive here. There is very limited non-resident parking, and it's pricey when it's available. Take the train, walk on the sand, guard your food like a hawk, and it's one of the nicest places you can get to in the summer without a car. Check the tide tables before you go, and expect to pay a small entrance fee.

Address 121 Beach Street, Manchester-by-the-Sea, MA 01944, +1 (978) 526-7276 (summer), www.manchester.ma.us/Facilities/Facility/Details/Singing-Beach-11 | **Getting there** Commuter Rail to Manchester-by-the-Sea (Newburyport/Rockport Line) | **Hours** See website for seasonal hours | **Tip** Between the commuter rail station and the beach is the brick and mortar shop selling the product that was featured in the first infomercial ever made: Saladmaster Cookware (48 Beach Street, Manchester-by-the-Sea, www.wecook.com for local shop).

98 The Skinny House

Home, petite home

And you thought your mother-in-law was petty. Also known as a "spite house," this narrow abode was allegedly built in the 1870s by a civil war soldier, who was dismayed upon returning home from battle to learn that his brother had already constructed a residence on the land their late father had left to them. So naturally, he did what any incensed sibling would: he built his own place directly behind it in order to block any sunlight from reaching his brother's home, a move that made for a pretty crummy view and not much room to live comfortably. Another less-circulated account purports The Skinny House to be the result of an argument between neighbors. Whatever the backstory, one thing is for sure: this house is skinnier than your favorite margarita.

Doing the tiny house thing way before it was trendy, this little dwelling measures just 10 feet wide by 30 feet deep, is four stories tall, and can only be entered through an alley. At 1,166 square feet, the home is actually more spacious by the numbers than many others in the neighborhood. Still, it would be an understatement to say that the interior is a bit tricky to navigate. From the narrow, freestanding metal and curved staircases to the built-in bunk beds and opposite walls you can touch with your arms outstretched, it's loaded with enough cramped quirks to make claustrophobic folks faint.

There *are* two ever-so-rare bits of outdoor space in the form of a roof deck with views of the harbor and North End, plus a small backyard with a patio. And despite being about a century-and-a-half old, The Skinny House has been outfitted with modern features, including a smart thermostat and storage solutions.

The privately-owned home, which most recently sold in September 2021 for $1.25 million, still garners a fair bit of attention, mainly from curious onlookers and nosy journalists hoping to get a peek inside.

Address 44 Hull Street, Boston, MA 02113 | Getting there Subway to Haymarket (Orange or Green Line) | Hours Unrestricted from the outside only | Tip Go see the O'Reilly Spite House too (260 Concord Avenue, Cambridge), a 308-square-foot residence built in 1908 as revenge during a feud between neighbors.

99 __ The Skull of Phineas Gage
A mind-altering experience

The next time you complain about having a bad day, think of poor Phineas Gage, a railroad construction worker who endured the unfortunate experience of having an iron rod completely penetrate his skull...and he lived to tell the tale. While working on the Rutland & Burlington Railroad in Vermont, Gage was preparing to blast some rock, a process that involved sprinkling gunpowder into holes and tamping it down with said rod.

Distracted by workers behind him, Gage turned his head. There's never been a verified account of exactly what happened to set it off, but the explosive powder ignited and sent the tamping iron hurtling through the foreman's cheekbone and through his skull. Shockingly, he never lost consciousness during the incident and was stable enough to stand up and settle into an oxcart for the trip to a nearby town. Reportedly, Gage joked with the doctor, "Here's business enough for you."

Sadly, things were never quite the same for Gage after that fateful day in 1848. Though he survived, the 27-year-old was rendered blind in his left eye, and his brain's left frontal lobe was severely damaged, transforming his personality for the remaining 12 years of his life. Many reported that the once hard-working, responsible man became "gross, profane, coarse, and vulgar." His friends described the new Phineas as "no longer Gage." Later, it's believed that his temperament began to even out, and his social skills began to return.

His fascinating story has been the subject of intense scrutiny in the medical community for decades, particularly in the field of neuroscience, the topic of cerebral localization, and the influence of the brain on one's personality and behavior. The skull – and the tamping iron – came to Boston in 1868, when Gage's former doctor John Martyn Harlow donated them to the Warren Anatomical Museum at the Countway Library.

Address Francis A. Countway Library of Medicine, 10 Shattuck Street, Boston, MA 02115, +1 (617) 432-6196, www.countway.harvard.edu/center-history-medicine/ warren-anatomical-museum | **Getting there** Subway to Brigham Circle (Green "E" Line) | **Hours** Mon–Fri 8am–11pm, Sat noon–7pm, Sun noon–11pm | **Tip** Experience a brain freeze of the temporary and delicious sort with an ice cream cone at JP Licks (1618 Tremont Street, One Brigham Circle, Boston, www.jplicks.com).

100__ SoWa Vintage Market
Bizarre bazaar

Every Sunday, rain or shine, this bazaar of delightfully bizarre knick-knacks, secondhand clothing, and vintage furniture takes over the basement of an antique brick warehouse building in the South End.

SoWa Vintage Market, named for Boston gallery district SoWa (short for "South of Washington"), where the market occurs, is special because its business model hits the sweet spot between "highly curated" and "extremely affordable for vendors" dead on. So the most creative, dedicated and competitive thrifters in the area come to the market to share their recent thrift scores. If they aren't showing new things in a creative and attractive display every week, they lose priority for their booths. So you can bet that every time you go, there will be new old things to turn over in your hands with wonder. And often completely different vendors from week to week.

The range of what you'll find here is wide, and what's for sale is ever changing. You never know whether you'll find regional vintage tchotchkes, elegant vintage dresses, kitchen implements that your grandmother's grandmother might have used, discretely homoerotic vintage oil paintings, or an almost-complete set of heavily used Rorschach test cards. (True story!)

In the colder weather, when much of the SoWa area's activity shuts down, SoWa Vintage Market does not. So when you venture out into the cold yourself, you'll often be rewarded with extra good deals, the great backstory of a particular treasure, or highly personalized fashion advice from a vintage collector. If you're in need of a vintage dealer in your life in an ongoing way, not just on Sundays, wintertime at SoWa Vintage Market is the time to cultivate that relationship.

But you should also visit in the summer because that's when the market bursts from its cold-weather basement and into large tents outside, surrounded by food trucks.

Address 450 Harrison Avenue, Boston, MA 02118, www.sowavintagemkt.com,
sowavintagemarket@gmail.com | **Getting there** Subway to Broadway (Red Line) or Tufts
Medical Center (Orange Line) | **Hours** Sun 10am–4pm, except Easter | **Tip** Come back to
SoWa for open gallery/studio night on the first Friday evening of every month, 5pm–9pm.
You'll hit an opening at every gallery and drop in on dozens of open studios
(450-460 Harrison Avenue, Boston, www.sowaboston.com/sowa-first-fridays).

101_ Swapfest: The Flea at MIT

Wondercabinet of obscure technology

The Swapfest at MIT is like no other flea market you've ever been to. Even if you're not planning to buy anything, it's worth visiting for the pure spectacle of it – and carrying a bit of cash just in case.

Afghans, furniture, knick-knacks and all things typical of flea markets are strictly forbidden here. But if you're looking for electronic parts of any kind – vintage or contemporary – this is the place to go. You can find the cameras, circuit boards, vintage video game controllers, or weird Russian vacuum tubes you're seeking, and at the best price possible. You can probably even pick up a new Enigma machine here if yours happens to be on the fritz. It's not guaranteed that someone will be selling one of these WWII encryption devices at Swapfest, but the chances are *significantly* higher here than at most other markets.

An Enigma machine is not even the coolest thing that Mitchell Berger, one of the current organizers of the monthly-during-good-weather event, has seen for sale during his tenure. That distinction goes to a Gemini space capsule. Not a model, not a toy, but an *actual* Gemini space capsule, one that had been used by NASA to train astronauts. You'd need a trailer to get it home.

Swapfest has been happening in a parking lot on MIT's campus for over 30 years now. It is run collaboratively by The MIT Radio Society, MIT UHF Repeater Association, the MIT Electronics Research Society, and the Harvard Wireless Club – all student HAM radio groups. Originally a multi-club fundraiser, Swapfest now draws specialized dealers, who often drive into town the night before to assure prime selling spots. Hundreds of electronics lovers descend as well, so make haste if you're hoping to snap up a used ultrasound machine or a theremin!

Address Albany Street Parking Garage, MIT Building N4, Cambridge, MA 02139, +1 (617) 253-3776, https://w1mx.mit.edu/flea-at-mit, w1mx-officers@mit.edu | Getting there Subway to Central (Red Line); bus 1 to Massachusetts Avenue & Albany Street | Hours Third Sun of each month, Apr–Oct, 9am–2pm | Tip Find The Infinite Corridor at MIT, an 825-foot passage through the main buildings on campus in a straight line, creating "MIThenge" when the sun glows through its entirety twice a year (enter at 77 Massachusetts Avenue, Cambridge).

102 Taza Chocolate Factory

You don't even need a golden ticket

There's chocolate and then there's chocolate. And if you're a chocolate lover, you love it all. Still, no matter how much chocolate you've had, there's a very strong chance that, unless you've spent some serious time in Mexico, you haven't had much of this style of chocolate.

Taza produces traditional Oaxacan-style stoneground chocolate, from the state of Oaxaca in Southwestern Mexico, at its Somerville factory. In 2005, the method was imported to the US by the company's co-founders Alex Whitmore and Kathleen Fulton, after Whitmore apprenticed with an Oaxacan *molinero* (chocolate miller) and learned to make his own granite millstones. It's these millstones, which Whitmore still makes by hand when they need replacing, that create the unique, stone-ground texture that Taza is famous for. But Taza has added another ingredient to their process that is equally important to its loyal customers: a guarantee that their products are produced from ethically sourced, fairly traded cacao beans. They even went so far as to establish a third-party Direct Trade Cacao Certification Program because no one else in the US had done so yet, and they felt it was critical to the work they were doing.

You can now find Taza chocolate in stores and cafés around the world. But if you love chocolate so much that you want to purchase everything they make – things like their chocolate-covered hazelnuts, the Honey Almond Dark Bark, the Wicked Dark Bar with Ginger, or the iconic Chipotle Chili Disc. You'll want to head to their factory store in Somerville. Don't forget (as if you'd forget!) to try all of the samples available while you're loading up your basket.

And if you love chocolate so much that you want to be completely surrounded by it, sign up in advance to take a 45-minute tour of Taza's factory. They make everything in their store right in Somerville, and you can watch and learn about the whole process, from bean to bar.

Address 561 Windsor Street, Somerville, MA 02143, +1 (617) 284-2232, www.tazachocolate.com | **Getting there** Subway to Central (Red Line), then a 20-minute walk; bus 69 to Cambridge Street & Columbia Street or bus 91 to Prospect Street & Webster Avenue | **Hours** See website for hours and tour schedule | **Tip** After Taza, stop by Somerville's community-run South Street Farm (198 South Street, Somerville, www.groundworksomerville.org/programs/south-street-farm).

103_ Tremont Temple

Ghosts of Dickens past

Take one look at the beautifully ornate exterior of Tremont Temple, a Baptist church, and you might not be too surprised to learn of the incredible moments that took place inside. The first Boston reading of the Emancipation Proclamation. Charles Dickens' first public reading of *A Christmas Carol*. A pre-presidency speech by Abraham Lincoln. A reading of *Uncle Tom's Cabin* by Harriet Beecher Stowe. At one point in 1850, there was even an Egyptian mummy on display. It might actually be less likely to hear about an event in 19th-century Boston that *didn't* happen at the Tremont Temple.

The church, which began as a playhouse theatre before being converted to a place of worship in 1843, has faced its share of adversity throughout the years. Three separate fires, in 1852, 1879, and 1893, burned the building to the ground. The current structure was built in 1896 by Clarence Blackall, whose work can also be seen at the nearby Emerson Colonial Theatre. From its beginning, the temple has held firm to key tenets, the most notable of which was, "…All who practice slavery or justify it, shall be excluded from the church and its communion…." As a result, it was home to the first integrated congregation in the country.

Despite all of its notable events and guests, Dickens' visit was especially exciting for Bostonians. When he arrived in town for the first time in 1842 and every time thereafter, residents rolled out the red carpet and treated him like the Beatles. Asking him to dinner, trying to break into his hotel room, even requesting locks of his hair – it was total Dickensmania!

There's a mirror on the second floor that's reportedly haunted by Dickens himself. It originally hung in a room at the Omni Parker House (see ch. 84), where the author stayed and practiced his reading of *A Christmas Carol,* complete with dramatic voices, in 1867.

Address 88 Tremont Street, Boston, MA 02108, +1 (617) 523-7320, www.tremonttemple.com | Getting there Subway to Park Street (Red or Green Line) or Government Center (Green or Blue Line) | Hours See website | Tip Another gorgeous, historic church, the first Anglican one in Boston, is steps away. King's Chapel, built in 1754, is adjacent to the oldest burial ground in the city (58 Tremont Street, Boston, www.kings-chapel.org).

104__Upper Allston
It's ALL in Allston!

Upper Allston, also known as "Harvard & Comm" (the intersection of Harvard and Commonwealth Avenues), is one of Boston's most eclectic and diverse neighborhoods. Crammed with small, cheap restaurants, bars hosting live music and DJs every night, and micro-businesses hawking everything from Brazilian football jerseys to Chinese herbal remedies, the local business council is not lying when it claims, "It's ALL in Allston!" And neither is the subculture that's dubbed this area "Allston, Rock City" because so many Boston bands have lived, rehearsed, and performed at small dank clubs in the area over decades. This intersection – and the blocks that stretch out in all four directions from it – also serves as Boston's unofficial Korea-town, a dining destination for local vegans, and a hub of Russian social activity and commerce.

There's a lot of turnover in the smaller storefronts, but a recent roam of a three-block radius of the intersection revealed: two record stores, five frozen confection shops, seventeen different types of ethnic food (Egyptian, El Salvadorean, Korean, Japanese, Vietnamese, Mexican, Brazilian, Italian, Indian, Afghan, Burmese, Chinese, Greek, Russian, Irish, Israeli, Turkish), three tattoo shops, three head shops, one weed store, three thrift stores, two bike repair shops, a shop that sells Wiccan things, an extremely busy guitar and amplifier shop, a pet shop, and hair salons specializing in taming four different kinds of ethnic hair.

Some of the larger stores that are local institutions include Bazaar, a Russian grocery; Hong Kong, a large pan-Asian market replete with crowded food court; and Blanchard's, a famous discount liquor store that supplies every college keg party in town.

Things change here all the time, and yet they always stay the same. It's always been a lively place to browse, flirt, people watch, rock out, or eat on the cheap, day or night.

Address Harvard & Commonwealth Avenues, Allston, MA 02134 | **Getting there** Subway
to Harvard Avenue (Green "B" Line) or Coolidge Corner (Green "C" Line); bus 66 to
Harvard Avenue & Commonwealth Avenue or bus 57 to Brighton Avenue & Linden Street |
Hours Unrestricted | **Tip** On the outside wall of The Silhouette Lounge, one of Upper
Allston's oldest old-school watering holes, look for an unusual city-sponsored mural:
a strange collage of non-average (i.e. famous) Joes (200 Brighton Avenue, Allston).

105 _ Victory Gardens
Blooming continuously since 1942

Victory Gardens, an idea developed by George Washington Carver, the most prominent Black scientist of the early 20th century, were used in tandem with rationing stamps to help preserve the national food supply during World War II. The idea was that by planting vegetable gardens at home and in public parks, people could supplement what was available in grocery stores, but also feel a sense of purpose and independence during a difficult wartime period. It is estimated that there were 20 million Victory Gardens at their peak, and that these were supplying more than 40% of the fresh fruits and vegetables consumed in the United States.

If the idea feels familiar, it's because Michelle Obama reprised it during her time as First Lady, starting a "kitchen garden" on the White House Lawn, as Eleanor Roosevelt did in 1942.

Public victory gardens are long gone, except for two: Dowling Community Garden in Minneapolis, and Fenway Victory Garden here in Boston. And these two are flourishing. Fenway, the only one that has operated continually since it was founded, has 500 individual gardens across more than seven acres. It's kept up by 475 gardeners representing every single neighborhood in the city. This urban gardening haven, lush with more flowers than vegetables now, also offers gardening workshops and hosts occasional festivals.

Part of Frederick Law Olmsted's famous park chain, the Emerald Necklace, this place is great for a meandering walk and for pretending that you're in the country rather than a city. Traffic and construction noises recede into the background as you stroll among the garden's diverse plots, smelling a flower here and inspecting a tomato there, chatting with Boston's most devoted earth-tillers. You can easily imagine what a refuge it was for those worried about loved ones on the front in the 1940s.

Address 1200 Boylston Street, Boston, MA 02215, www.fenwayvictorygardens.org, info@fenwayvictorygardens.org | Getting there Subway to Fenway (Green "D" Line) | Hours Daily dawn–dusk | Tip Also in the Fens area of the Emerald Necklace is a 450-pound, almost 350-year-old bell from a Buddhist temple in Japan, given to Boston as a symbol of reconciliation after WWII (25 The Fenway, Boston, www.emeraldnecklace.org).

106__ Vilna Shul

Jews that go way back

Boston, like all of the United States, has been shaped via wave after wave of immigration from other parts of the world. Boston has the third-largest population of Haitians outside of Haiti and the largest population of Brazilian immigrants in the entire US. In fact, of the 50 largest cities in the US, Boston ranks sixth in terms of ethnic diversity. Some cultures (read Irish) are just much more visible (and celebrated by films set here) than others. Though it's not well commemorated, we've also had Jewish migration to Boston since 1649.

The largest waves of Jewish immigration here occurred in the late 1800s and through the early 20th century. In 1907, there were 60,000 Jews in Boston, about 10% of the city's population. By 1920 these impoverished families, fleeing pogroms and persecution in Eastern and Central Europe with whatever they could carry, had pooled their resources to build over 50 synagogues in the city.

Most of these institutions are gone now, but one still stands and plays a vibrant role in Boston's Jewish community's life: Vilna Shul. Located in now-tony but once tenement-filled Beacon Hill, Vilna Shul is a simple, L-shaped building which was in rough shape for many years, but has recently undergone major renovations. Today, it is filled with light from its soaring skylights and tall stained glass windows.

Take guided or audio tours that relate its unique history, or check out challenging work by local artists, such as their recent exhibition, "Holding Differences Tenderly." The artist Brenda Bancel collaborated with high school students Toni Marie Gomes and Roody Jean Louis to communicate their perceptions of inherent bias through photography.

The temple, the only one in Boston on the state's registry of historic places, and the oldest Jewish historic landmark in the city, also offers a variety of lectures and social gatherings, open to all.

Address 18 Phillips Street, Boston, MA 02114, +1 (617) 523-2324, www.vilnashul.org, info@vilnashul.org | Getting there Subway to Charles/MGH (Red Line), Park Street (Green or Red Line), or Bowdoin (Blue Line) | Hours See website hours and events | Tip For more Beacon Hill history, amble down to the Nichols House Museum (55 Mt. Vernon Street, Boston, www.nicholshousemuseum.org), a preserved 1804 townhouse that was the former residence of suffragist and pacifist Rose Standish Nichols and her family.

107_Wally's Jazz Club

Let's talk about sax, baby

When it comes to live jazz, Wally's is one of the last bastions for it in Boston, and it's among the oldest of its kind in the entire country. Joseph Walcott, an immigrant from Barbados, became the first Black nightclub owner in New England when he opened the club as Wally's Paradise in 1947 at 428 Massachusetts Avenue. The venue moved across the street in 1979, but hardly anything else has changed. You don't even need to close your eyes to imagine how things used to be. It remains the oldest family-owned jazz club in the country, as Walcott's children and grandchildren have continued to manage it since he passed away in 1998.

Sitting quite unassumingly amongst rows of brick brownstones in the South End, Wally's bright red door is the only exterior indication that there's something quite exciting happening behind it. Unfortunately, many other Boston venues that helped to bring jazz to the city, like Hi-Hat and Chicken Lane, are no longer around. So Wally's represents both the past and future, as it preserves the best parts of that golden era while celebrating new artists from around the area and the country and introducing the genre to younger generations.

Since its inception, Wally's has served as a training ground for student musicians from nearby Berklee College of Music and the New England Conservatory of Music. It's also hosted renowned musicians, including Billie Holiday, Art Blakey, Charlie Parker, and Esperanza Spalding. It's this diverse range of programming that makes the small space so special. And it operates 365 nights a year, offering improvisational jam sessions and polished performances of jazz, blues, funk, and salsa, depending on the night. But don't expect velvet ropes and mixologists. There's a full bar, but the atmosphere here is wonderfully bare-bones and intimate, with the focus where it should be: squarely on the music.

Address 427 Massachusetts Avenue, Roxbury, MA 02118, +1 (617) 424-1408, www.wallyscafe.com | **Getting there** Subway to Massachusetts Avenue (Orange Line) or Symphony (Green "E" Line) | **Hours** See website for hours and events | **Tip** If you're feeling inspired by the virtuosos on stage, stop by Music Espresso to pick up some sheet music and hone your own skills (33 Gainsborough Street, No. 106, Boston, www.musicespresso.com).

108__ Washington Tower

From six feet under to 125 feet above

Psst! Can you keep a secret? If so, here's one for you: you'll find one of the best views of Boston from smack-dab in the middle of a graveyard. All you have to do is pick a day when the sky is clear and climb to the top of a tower.

Built between 1852 and 1854 at the highest point in Mount Auburn Cemetery, Washington Tower was constructed as a memorial to the first US president, George Washington. It was designed by cemetery president Jacob Bigelow and architect Gridley James Fox Bryant, who also worked on the original Charles Street Jail (see ch. 70). The structure, built with local Quincy granite blocks, stands at 62 feet tall. Its design was heavily influenced by medieval architecture – look for its spiral staircase, Gothic windows, and battlements.

Go much further back in time, and it seems the spot where Washington Tower stands has always had geological significance in the area that became Boston. The tower sits atop a natural hill shaped in a way that suggests it is a kame, a sediment deposit formed by streams running on top of glacial ice. If you climb the 90 steps to the top and look to the North (find North by looking for Bigelow Chapel, another gothic-looking structure built from the same Quincy granite), you can still trace the pathway of what was once a glacial valley running from Winchester Highlands towards where the tower stands. The modern roadways still echo its ancient route.

Squint a bit, and you can alternate between imagining the area's deepest, ice-age past and taking in panoramic bird's-eye views of Boston's elegant skyline, the winding Charles River, the gold-domed State House, and nearby Harvard University.

Or you can just re-enact your favorite tower-based fairytale fantasies. Along with breathtaking views of Boston, this is the perfect place for your quest to slay a dragon or to play Rapunzel.

Address Mount Auburn Cemetery, Mountain Avenue, Watertown, MA 02472,
+1 (617) 547-7105, www.mountauburn.org, info@mountauburn.org | Getting there
Bus 71 or 73 to Mount Auburn Street & Coolidge Avenue | Hours Daily 8am–6pm |
Tip There are as many stories in Mount Auburn Cemetery as there are graves, so once you've
had your fill of the view from the tower, climb down and explore! See if you can find Kittie
Knox, Black suffragist and cyclist, on Vesper Path (www.mountauburn.org/aaht-knox).

109 Woody's L Street Tavern

I guess I'll have two more of these

Chances are high that Gus Van Sant's 1997 film *Good Will Hunting* has shaped your sense of the city's charms, whether you live here or you're visiting. So you owe it to yourself to go at least once to have a quiet beer – or three – at the bar featured in the movie. Ideally, you should watch it a day or so before and then do a self-guided tour of all of the Boston spots where it was filmed. Make sure to end here because it's perfect.

Despite all of the attention the bar has received since being featured in the film, and the slight facelift it's had since, Woody's L Street Tavern is exactly what it always has been: a cozy neighborhood watering hole, with true Irish hospitality. It's so old-school, it didn't have a website until 2021!

It's bright here because its windows wrap around a sunny corner, with a warm, wood-trimmed interior. So you'll understand immediately why Van Sant fell so in love with Woody's while location scouting that he scrapped his original plan to shoot the bar scenes on a Canadian sound stage to save money. You'll also understand why the site brought out the absolute best in local actors Ben Affleck and Matt Damon – there's no way they couldn't have felt truly at home in this quintessentially Boston bar.

If you're hoping to grab the exact table where Affleck and Damon and their characters' buddies hung out in the film, that's completely possible – it's hard to miss because stills from the film now adorn its high-gloss surface. But if it's already taken, rest assured you'll be treated well no matter where you sit. Just refrain from retelling the joke Minnie Driver's character tells in the movie about the Irishman and the genie. Even though, yes, Guinness is an incredible beverage, and it's nothing but wise to want to order extra glasses to drink with your friends, everyone's heard that one already.

Address 658 East 8th Street, South Boston, MA 02127, +1 (617) 268-4335, https://woodyslstreet.com | Getting there Bus 11 to East 8th Street & L Street | Hours Wed–Sun noon–1am, Mon–Tue 4pm–1am | Tip It goes without saying that this is the place to be on St. Patrick's Day in Boston, it's pretty impossible to get in on St. Patrick's Day. Wanna up your chances? Take Irish clogging lessons at Woods Irish Dance School (479 East 7th Street, Boston, www.woodsirishdance.com) a few blocks away – their students almost always perform at the bar on St. Paddy's Day.

110_ You Do It Electronics
DIY overload

How geeky are you? Are you geeky enough to know the birthday of the Arduino microcontroller? If so, you need to know about You Do It Electronics immediately, and you'll want to make your way there every April because they'll probably be the only place in town hosting an annual birthday party to celebrate the open source software/hardware system. Come here for some pretty unique fun with lots of beeping and buzzing, and automated things skittering around underfoot. And chortling. Lots of chortling.

Even if you have not just run out of solder in the middle of making your own 3D printer or robot or guitar effects pedal at home, You Do It is worth a visit. Where else could you browse 57 different kinds of flashlights before settling on the ECLIPSE X-Spot Handheld Spotlight that will make every trip to your basement to flip a circuit breaker feel like a spy mission from now on?

You Do It is kind of a micro-tech superstore (though they have plenty of macro tech too). It's a fascinating place to visit even if you have no idea what anything is. But if you do want to know what something is, you're in luck: the You Do It team has been at this for over 70 years. They are super friendly and knowledgeable, and they often host in-store showcases or workshops to lure you into the world of taking things apart and putting them together again better or weirder. Ever wanted to know how to make your own Swiss Army knife? They'll show you how. Ditto making your own Tesla coil.

And that's just the kid stuff.

If you're an adult, maybe it's time to figure out how to make your work-from-home teleconferences look as good as HD television. Or maybe integrate LEDs into your cycling clothing for added safety. Or make your doorbell into a video camera that streams straight to your mobile phone. You Do It can help you do it all.

Address 40 Franklin Street, Needham, MA 02494, +1 (781) 449-1005, www.youdoitelectronics.com, sales@youdoitelectronics.com | **Getting there** Subway to Newton Highlands (Green "D" Line), transfer to bus 59 to Needham Street & Oak Street | **Tip** While you're in the area, stop by one of the biggest branches of Boston's amazing Russian supermarket chain, Bazaar. They've got everything from caviar by the pound, to obscure Eastern European homeopathic remedies (30 Tower Road, Newton, www.bazaarsupermarkets.com).

111 ZUMIX

Not your average after-school program

From its humble beginnings in 1991 as a summer songwriting program for just 24 participants, ZUMIX was birthed from an immediate need to curb widespread youth violence in the East Boston neighborhood. The hope was that if the kids were provided a positive outlet for their energy, their lives and the community would benefit as a result. Fast forward nearly 30 years, and ZUMIX is a full-fledged paradise for creative pursuits, serving more than 1,000 students every year through a combination of courses at its own facility and in-school partnerships. In fact, the name ZUMIX was coined in 1993 by a kid in one of the programs, and the organization has since defined it as a noun that means both "music, crafted and shared by everyone" and "a family."

ZUMIX is housed in a space that's just as cool as the organization is: the former Engine Company 40 Firehouse, which sat vacant for more than three decades before the organization arrived in 2010. More technical classes in audio production, beatmaking, and studio recording complement sessions that focus on fundamentals of songcraft and performance, providing a holistic experience for both aspiring and accomplished musicians. Participants even have the opportunity to turn their dreams into reality by honing their radio DJ skills and broadcasting live on 94.9FM.

Beyond these enrichment programs, the organization has become a unifying fixture in the community, hosting outdoor concerts, in-house movie screenings, festivals, and open mic nights that draw around 10,000 people every year.

While the bulk of the programming here is geared toward area youth, grown-ups can take beginner lessons in everything from guitar and piano to bass and ukulele through an initiative called Play It Forward. Tuition goes toward ensuring that youth programs remain subsidized or free, so you're simultaneously doing good and rocking out.

Address 260 Sumner Street, East Boston, MA 02128, +1 (617) 568-9777, www.zumix.org, info@zumix.org | Getting there Subway to Maverick (Blue Line); bus 120 to Sumner Street & Orleans Street | Hours See website for current programming. | Tip While in Eastie, you simply have to grab a New York-style slice at Santarpio's (111 Chelsea Street, Boston, www.santarpiospizza.com), a cash-only spot that's beloved by locals and tourists alike.

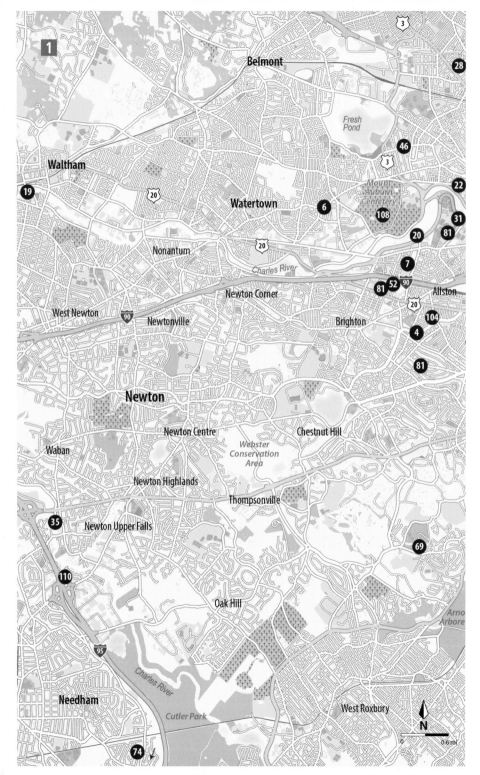

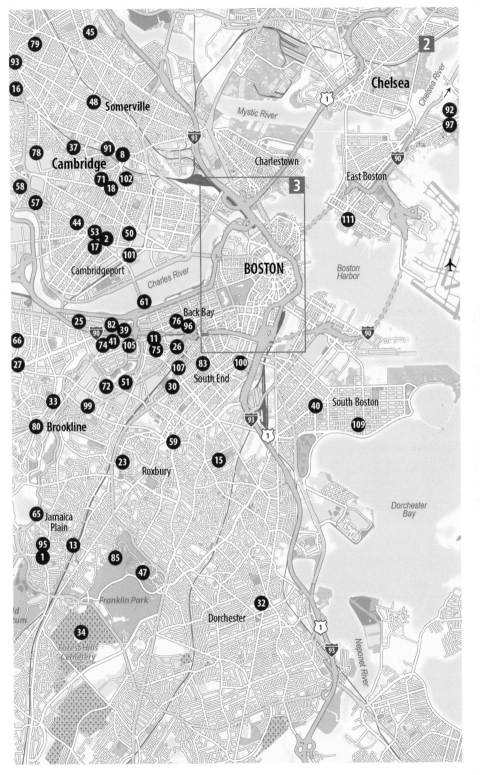

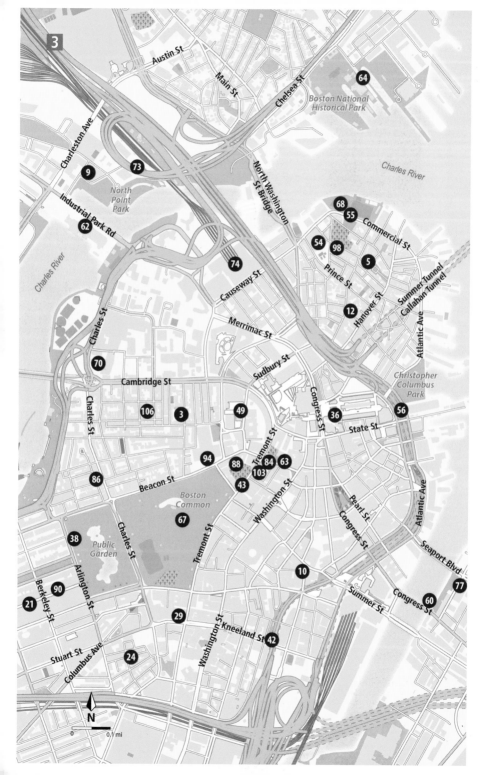

Jo-Anne Elikann
111 Places in New York
That You Must Not Miss
ISBN 978-3-95451-052-8

Wendy Lubovich, Jean Hodgens
111 Places in the Hamptons
That You Must Not Miss
ISBN 978-3-7408-0751-1

Wendy Lubovich, Ed Lefkowicz
111 Museums in New York
That You Must Not Miss
ISBN 978-3-7408-0379-7

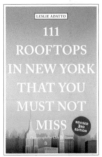

Leslie Adatto, Clay Williams
111 Rooftops in New York
That You Must Not Miss
ISBN 978-3-7408-0905-8

John Major, Ed Lefkowicz
111 Places in Brooklyn
That You Must Not Miss
ISBN 978-3-7408-0380-3

Kevin C. Fitzpatrick, Joe Conzo
111 Places in the Bronx
That You Must Not Miss
ISBN 978-3-7408-0492-3

Joe DiStefano, Clay Williams
111 Places in Queens
That You Must Not Miss
ISBN 978-3-7408-0020-8

Andréa Seiger, John Dean
111 Places in Washington
That You Must Not Miss
ISBN 978-3-7408-0258-5

Allison Robicelli, John Dean
111 Places in Baltimore
That You Must Not Miss
ISBN 978-3-7408-0158-8

Amy Bizzarri, Susie Inverso
111 Places in Chicago
That You Must Not Miss
ISBN 978-3-7408-1030-6

Michelle Madden, Janet McMillan
111 Places in Milwaukee
That You Must Not Miss
ISBN 978-3-7408-0491-6

Elisabeth Larsen
111 Places in the Twin Cities
That You Must Not Miss
ISBN 978-3-7408-1347-5

Sandra Gurvis, Mitch Geiser
111 Places in Columbus
That You Must Not Miss
ISBN 978-3-7408-0600-2

Cristyle Egitto, Jakob Takos
111 Places in Palm Beach
That You Must Not Miss
ISBN 978-3-7408-1452-6

Gordon Streisand
111 Places in Miami and the
Keys That You Must Not Miss
ISBN 978-3-95451-644-5

Travis Swann Taylor
111 Places in Atlanta
That You Must Not Miss
ISBN 978-3-7408-0747-4

Dana DuTerroil, Joni Fincham,
Daniel Jackson
111 Places in Houston
That You Must Not Miss
ISBN 978-3-7408-0896-9

Kelsey Roslin, Nick Yeager,
Jesse Pitzler
111 Places in Austin
That You Must Not Miss
ISBN 978-3-7408-0748-1

Art Credits

SCUL Bike Shop at Artisan's Asylum (ch. 7): Various artists
Catastrophe Cake (ch. 13): Caitlin & Misha, artists
(aka Caitlin Foley and Misha Rabinovich)
Boston Hassle Flea: (ch. 14): Bruce Sainte, artist
Dorchester Art Project (ch. 32): Spion: Graphic Prints,
"Brandie Blaze, Red Shade, and Oompa," photographed
by Leonardo Claudio from Leographic Photography LLC
from his 2018 Solo Exhibition UNAPOLOGETIC:
Celebrating activists in the Music Scene
Friend Smithsonian Museum (ch. 48): Martha Friend, artist
Ibis Ascending (ch. 49): Judy Kensley McKie, sculptor
Graffiti Alley (ch. 53): Various artists
The Harvard Square Theater Mural (ch. 58): Joshua Winer,
designer and painter, 1985
Andrew Jackson Figurehead (ch. 64): USS *Constitution's*
Andrew Jackson Figurehead made by Charles Wetherill (1834)
and a carved wooden mouthpiece from the original figurehead
by Laban S. Beecher (1834)
Jamaica Pond Bench (ch. 65): Matthew Hincman, artist
Under the Hill (ch. 71): Dan Masi, artist
Boston Marathon Memorial (ch. 76): Pablo Eduardo, sculptor
Museum of Modern Renaissance (ch. 79): Nicholas Shaplyko
and Ekaterina Sorokina, artist
Self Portrait (ch. 88): Polly Thayer Starr, artist
The Puppeteers' Cooperative presents: The Puppet Free Library (ch.90):
The Puppet Free Library, creators
Triumph of Religion (ch. 96): John Singer Sargent, artist

There are a lot of unknowns in a first-time collaboration even when the world – and world traveling – is *not* paused indefinitely by an extremely contagious virus. Kim, Alyssa, and Emons' editor Karen Seiger all surfed these strange waves with grace and helped me to do the same. I'll also shout out here to the Boston gems we had to exclude in this round because their reopening dates were not firmed up enough: I'm rooting for each of them to be showcased in future editions. And finally, I'd like to evoke the memory of my parents here, who decided (more or less on a whim) that Boston would be a better place to have kids than NYC.

Heather Kapplow

I'd like to thank Heather and Alyssa for being such fantastic writing and photography partners as we worked through the challenges of creating a guidebook during a pandemic, and our editor Karen Seiger, for supporting us the whole way through! I'm also grateful to everyone from our 111 places who shared their stories and time to help us make this project a reality in the midst of so much uncertainty. Lastly, I have to credit the late, great Anthony Bourdain for inspiring my passion for exploring the world.

Kim Windyka

I started my photography career here in Boston and it has been an amazing experience to honor this wonderful city in the way of photographing this book. This project would not be possible without this hardworking and dedicated Boston team. I have to thank and praise Kim and Heather and their beautiful writing and for tirelessly helping me connect with all our 111 locations. To Karen Seiger, for keeping us on schedule and pushing us along this entire year. And of course to the city of Boston as a whole, for persevering, and reinventing itself all while keeping its wildly unique vibe. Oh, Boston, you're my home.

Alyssa Wood

Heather Kapplow (www.heatherkapplow.com) is one of the rarest kind of creatures you'll find in Boston: a native Bostonian. A visual and performing artist as well as a writer, Heather travels frequently for projects in both spheres and has a very deep understanding of what it's like to be a newcomer in an unfamiliar city. (Exciting, but it can also take forever to find the cool stuff if you don't know any insiders…) It's among Heather's life goals to make Boston a more welcoming place, as well as to throw spotlights on Boston's many nuanced subcultures. You can find anything you need in Boston (except maybe a parking space in the winter) if you seek it out—take it from a native.

Kim Windyka fell in love with Boston while growing up in nearby southern New Hampshire, and has never tired of the city's beauty and historic charm in the years she's been living here since attending Emerson College. A full-time copywriter with experience in multiple industries including travel, tech, and fashion, she has also written pieces for *The Atlantic*, *New York Magazine*, *McSweeney's*, and more. See more of her work at www.kimwindyka.com and follow her on Twitter at @kimlw.

Alyssa Wood is a New England based photographer specializing in event and documentary photography. She is a graduate of New England School of Photography graduating with a major of portrait and editorial photography and spent four years living and photographing in Boston. She now lives in Rhode Island with her husband two kids, Bella & Sam and enjoys grabbing a coffee and relaxing by the beach and travels to Boston frequently for work and pleasure.